LONGMAN
TUTORIAL
RESOURCES

This book to be returned on or before the last date stamped below.

Headteacher, Nort

Head of Continui

370

6

Alison Leake
& Andrew Leake

CONTENTS

Know yourself

Relationships

Being a sixth former

CONTENTS

A NEW START IN THE SIXTH

For many students the sixth form presents an opportunity to leave a younger self behind and move in a new direction. The assignments below let you think about your attitude to your teachers and your tutor, in the past and now in the sixth form. It is also a useful exercise at the beginning of the school year when you may need to get to know a new Tutor Group.

ASSIGNMENTS ▷ ▷ ▷ ▷ ▷ ▷ ▷ ▷

1 When you have read the piece about 'Mrs Brown', work out why the student remembers this teacher so vividly. What might she have done to help him/her?

2 In a group take it in turns to describe an experience in your own schooling that you remember with pleasure.

3 Now you are in the sixth form, how do you think a teacher's role may differ from that earlier in your education? How may you have to adapt?

4 Imagine a scene in the sixth form similar to that described in the article. Role-play in pairs to devise techniques that would help (a) a teacher and (b) a tutor to help you.

Pain that lingers

Mrs Brown

Why is it that we remember the horrid teachers in our lives, and not the good ones? I had one of the former variety in my reception year at school and I'm sure she influenced my ability to learn. In fact it is probably only now, as I start my college life, that I feel free of her.

I'll call her Mrs Brown. Really I wonder why she stayed in teaching. She had no awareness of how a child feels, let alone learns. What I remember most was when I was stuck on a problem with sums. The problem just made no sense. I raised my arm and asked her to help. She was very impatient. 'I'll show you again,' she sighed, emphasising the last word.

This made me panic, and I remember being close to tears. When she passed my desk again, she looked down at my page, and threw the book into the corner of the room. 'You're so stupid,' she yelled. The rest of the class stared at me. That was what really hurt.

ENJOYING GOOD TIMES

Too often in life we remember 'the bad times'. Yet there is so much to enjoy about living. The activities here should be enjoyable in themselves, but they also act as an 'ice breaker' if you are in a new Tutor Group.

Five Years Old

Five-year-olds dream of becoming giants –
Golden-bearded, striding around the map,
Gulping streams, munching sandwiches
Of crushed ice and white-hot anthracite
Between two slices of slate.
They sit on the edge of Salisbury Plain
Bawling huge songs across the counties
For ten days at a time,
Eating trees, cuddling carthorses,
Before stomping home to Windsor Castle.
They name clouds. They fall in love with buses,
They lick the stars, they are amazed by hoses,
They dance all the time because they don't think about dancing . . .

They long to be allowed into the big good schools
Which will teach them to be giants with wings.

Adrian Mitchell

ASSIGNMENTS ▷ ▷ ▷ ▷ ▷ ▷ ▷ ▷

1 Bring in photos of yourself at about five years old. What can you remember about the good times (a) of your childhood? (b) of last year?

2 What can we learn from five-year-olds about enjoying life? How could you achieve the last line of Adrian Mitchell's poem?

ENJOYING GOOD TIMES

Enjoying life

ENJOYING GOOD TIMES

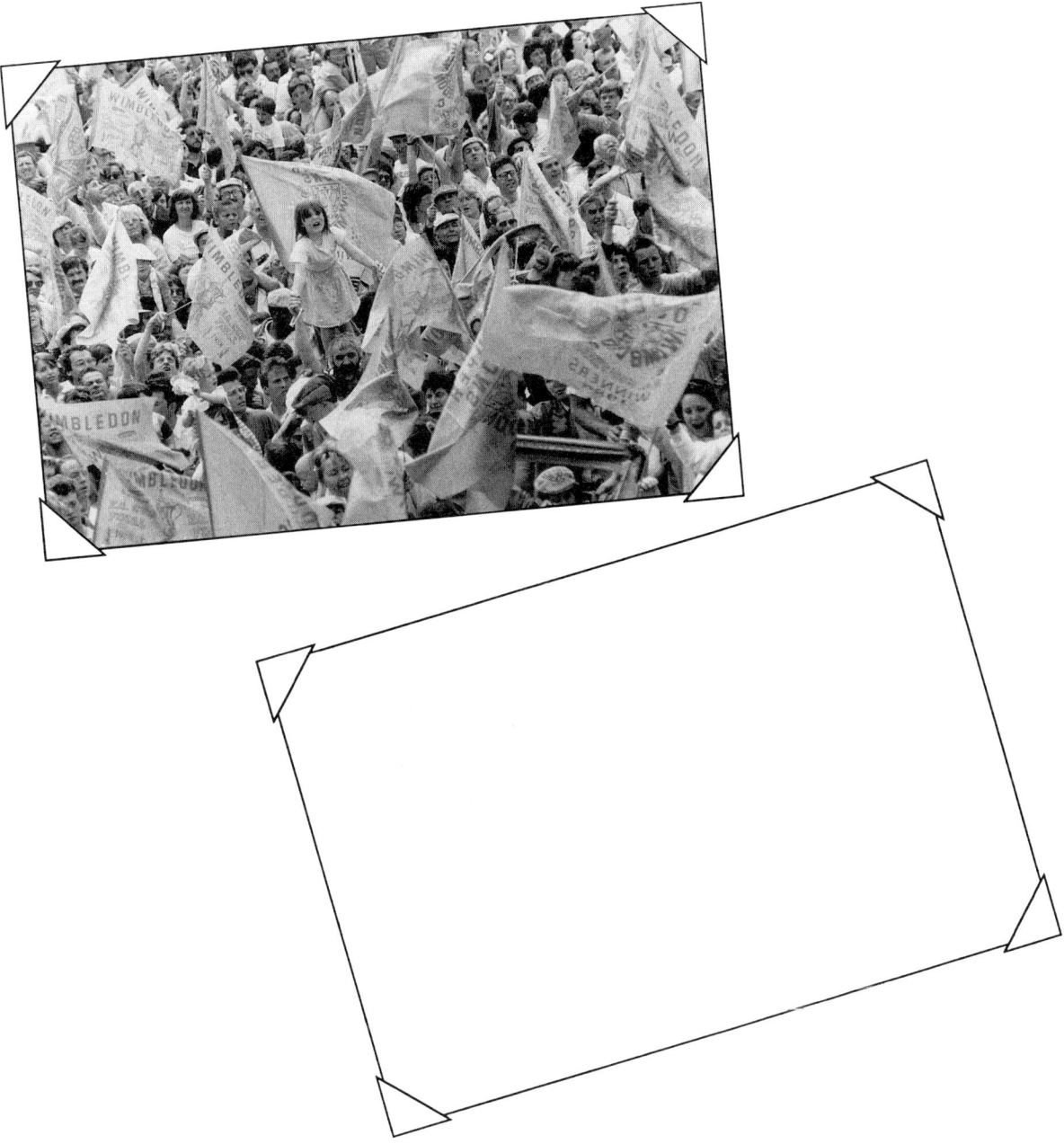

ASSIGNMENTS ▷ ▷ ▷ ▷ ▷ ▷ ▷ ▷ ▷

1 With which photo do you identify most?

2 What would you put in the blank space for one of your friends or family?

3 How would your 'good time' be represented in a new photo 'snapshot'?

4 Compare your 'snapshot' with others. What similarities or differences do you notice?

COPING WITH BAD TIMES

Help yourself – how can you set about turning bad times into good? One device that may be useful in sorting out a specific problem is a forcefield such as the one below. It aims to show all the important issues and to balance points for or against solving the 'problem'. The different lengths of the arrows signify their power. This framework may help you to anticipate and overcome difficulties in your way.

A problem-solving forcefield

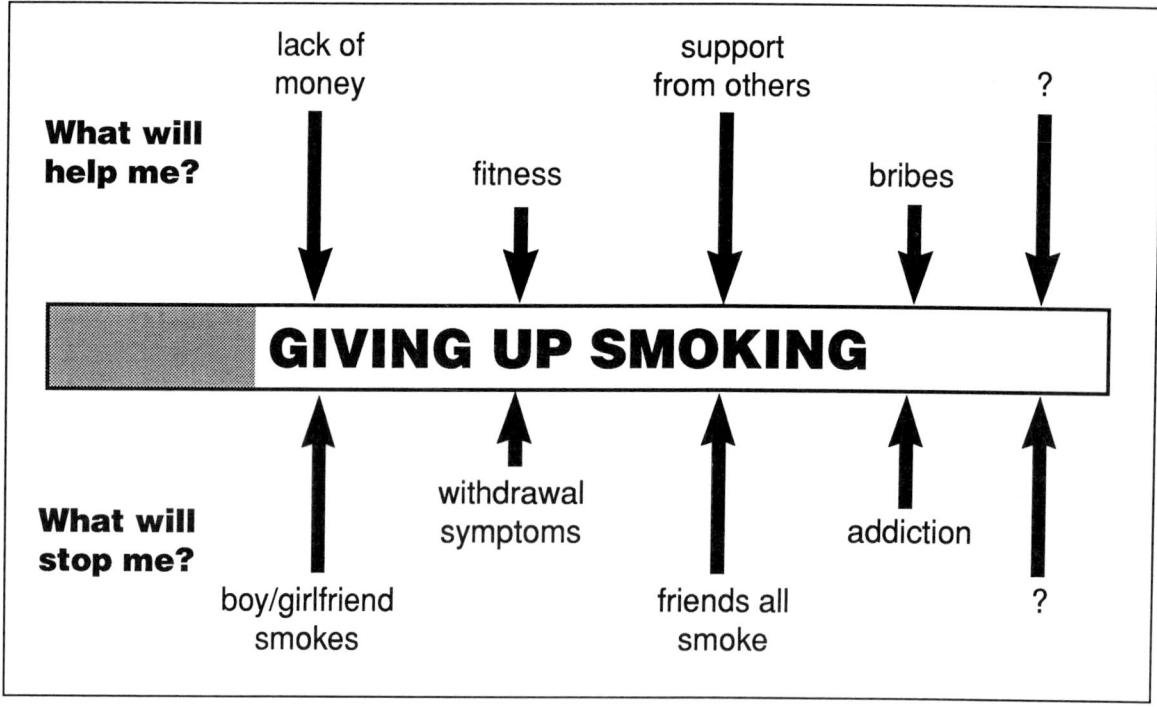

lack of money | support from others | ?

What will help me?

fitness | bribes

GIVING UP SMOKING

What will stop me?

withdrawal symptoms | addiction

boy/girlfriend smokes | friends all smoke | ?

ASSIGNMENTS ▷ ▷ ▷ ▷ ▷ ▷ ▷ ▷

1 Discuss possible labels for the two unmarked arrows, and the relative strengths of the others, in the forcefield for giving up smoking.

2 Think of a goal you would like to reach this term. After you have drawn the relevant forcefield, discuss it with a friend.

COPING WITH BAD TIMES

3 In pairs, role-play a scene in which you take a problem to a particular support service. These are examples but you may prefer to invent your own:

- asking your parent/guardian if you can have a place in the home where you can work in quiet;
- asking your family doctor about contraceptives;
- asking your tutor to arrange an extension for a subject teacher's project.

4 What makes life stressful for you? Collect suggestions in a group, just writing them down at first without discussion. After this 'brainstorming session' choose one suggestion that you all share and talk about ways of recognising it and handling it. (See 'Stress', page 108.)

5 The 'Agony Hat' game is useful for getting ideas to help with a problem. Everyone writes down on a slip of paper a current worry. These are then placed in a hat or box. Members of the group take turns to draw out a slip and respond as an agony aunt might.

Saying no

It is difficult for most people to say 'NO', to refuse, to disagree. Being negative can make us feel guilty and unhelpful, especially if parents or guardians have brought us up to be cooperative and caring towards others. But there is no need to feel guilty about being true to your own feelings. Here are two activities that help you practise disagreeing with others, saying 'no', and receiving 'no' too.

ASSIGNMENTS ▷ ▷ ▷ ▷ ▷ ▷ ▷ ▷

1 Take it in turns, in groups of six or seven, to be the person who disagrees. The rest of the group quietly decide on two consecutive numbers. They then 'clap out' one of the numbers, but do not recite the numbers at the same time. At the end of their clapping, they all call out the other number, for example, they may clap six times, but call out 'seven'. The person who disagrees has to count the claps and say the number she or he hears, for example, in this case, 'six'. Repeat the activity a few times with each person playing the part of the person who disagrees.

Discuss afterwards how you felt being in disagreement.

2 This activity is sometimes called a 'fishbowl'. Half the members of the group form a circle back to back. The rest of the group face them, forming an outer circle. This group has to make a persistent request, and the inner partner in each case refuses. The outer group moves on after two minutes to face a new partner and repeat the request. It must still be met by refusal by the inner partner. Continue until everyone has 'partnered' each other. You can vary the requests as you go round, but the answer must always be 'no'!

Discuss afterwards how you felt making constant refusals.

Finally, discuss ways of coping with saying 'no', refusing, and disagreeing.

Values that left a rape victim so vulnerable

HARRIET had been brought up to believe in old fashioned virtues – to be polite, to care for others, to fit in rather than stand out from the crowd.

David, the student she met at her prestigious college, was a former minor public schoolboy who, like her, had come from a middle class home.

He had the same values. In every way a suitable first serious boyfriend.

Harriet's mother, a teacher, therefore saw nothing to worry about when the two 18-year-olds set off on a sponsored 24-hour hitch-hike across Europe raising cash for charity at so much a mile.

But the nightmare which the Christmas vacation turned into made a mockery of the code Harriet and David were raised to respect.

Indeed, if either had come from a different background, trained like streetwise children to trust no one and regard strangers bearing gifts with suspicion, it may never have happened at all.

Convinced

Such youngsters would have reacted differently to the events of January 7 when Harriet and David, long since split up from the seven other college couples on the charity drive, thumbed a lift outside Annecy, 500 miles from Paris.

Two well-dressed Frenchmen in their 20s offered a ride in a Skoda to the best spot for hitching Paris-bound lorries.

The young innocents accepted and also went along with the suggestion of a drink in Annecy with the friendly Frenchmen.

'I thought it was a bit strange but because David and I were together we said yes to the offer,' explained Harriet back in her comfortable university rooms last week.

All four went to a café where Harriet, at the two Frenchmen's bidding, settled for a Coke and Malibu.

David drank beer and the new-found friends introduced themselves as Patrick and Hervé. In the café they all played table-football, Patrick saying he found blonde and leggy Harriet very beautiful indeed. David, sure in his love, did not react.

After a couple of hours Hervé announced he was going home and Patrick invited the two students to travel with him through the snowy night to the start of the main Paris road. For the first time Harriet began to fear something was wrong as she saw road signs for Paris pointing in a different direction.

But she convinced herself, in her well-mannered way, that she was just being silly, that if she spoke out she would offend Patrick who was, after all, doing her and David a favour.

Manipulate

'The first thing that really scared me after that was the route Patrick was taking, up hairpin bends on an icy mountain road,' she said.

'As we climbed higher the conditions worsened but he just said he was taking a short cut.'

Then Harriet and David fell for a simple trick less trusting young people would have seen through. 'Patrick explained that his car battery was running down. I thought he was joking, until he started to turn the vehicle round and asked David to get out to help push,' said Harriet.

Like the gentleman he was, reared to be, David instantly obliged. But as he stood in the snow at the side of the Skoda the Frenchman suddenly drove off with Harriet in the car.

David, an engineering student who is still visibly shaken at the ordeal, says today: 'I still wonder why I got out of that car to help.

'I suppose I felt we owed this Frenchman a favour. I mean, there were two of us against him but he still managed to manipulate us. Basically, we trusted him.'

Patrick pulled into a mountain lay-by and turned off the engine and lights.

'He moved towards me. I screamed and he raised his fist,' recalls Harriet.

'I made a decision there and then not to fight him.'

Harriet was raped swiftly and brutally.

'Thinking back,' she says now, 'perhaps David and I should have left Patrick earlier. But when you believe someone is doing you a good turn I am very loathe to be rude to them.'

'Basically we trusted him'

COPING WITH BAD TIMES

After the rape Harriet was dropped back at the spot where she had left David. The couple immediately reported her ordeal to the police and the man who called himself Patrick – a false name – was charged.

Now Harriet and David face returning to France to give evidence against the man who has claimed that Harriet welcomed his advances and fabricated the rape story to pacify David.

The students will have to prove this cruel lie is untrue before her attacker is put behind bars.

At the initial judicial hearing at the local Palais de Justice the woman judge made Harriet stand side by side with 'Patrick' and commented that since the English girl was taller than the rapist she could have fought him off.

Understand

The seeds of doubt have been sown and they may ultimately allow 'Patrick' to have his freedom.

The question now is will the French courts understand how the British middle class still bring up their children?

Will those who have to make the decision about whether Harriet was raped on a freezing French night in January understand that rightly or wrongly she was taught to trust?

'I want to warn others like David and me not to fall into the same trap,' she says.

'That man is guilty and my only crime was to believe that, like others in my life, he was a friend.'

ASSIGNMENTS ▷ ▷ ▷ ▷ ▷ ▷ ▷ ▷

1 In pairs work out the issues raised in this article.

2 What are the solutions?

From Sarah Tyne in *Mail on Sunday*, 20 March 1988

TAKING CHARGE

Learning to express your views and ideas to other people involves learning a form of communication that also respects their viewpoint and feelings. It is all too easy to upset someone by responding in an **aggressive** manner to another person's suggestion. On the other hand, you can be **passive** and avoid a conflict, but be upset that you haven't expressed yourself clearly, if at all. As this assignment will show you, it pays to learn to be **assertive**, that is direct but not disrespectful.

What would you say?

A father asks his son to wash up. A boy asks a girl to go to a party with him. These are common scenarios. Think of some scenarios from your own experience and consider differing responses.

ASSIGNMENTS ▷ ▷ ▷ ▷ ▷ ▷ ▷ ▷

1 You have masses of homework but your father/guardian asks you to wash up. What do you say?
   - 'Why don't you do them? Can't you see how much work I've got?'
   - 'All right Dad.'
   - 'Can't I do my turn tomorrow, Dad? I've got so much homework tonight.'

2 You've been asked to a party by someone you don't want to go out with. What do you say?
   - 'Get lost!'
   - 'Sorry, I'm already going out that night.'
   - 'Thanks for asking, but I'd rather not.'

TAKING CHARGE

What are you like?

	5	4	3	2	1	
appearance oriented	.	.	.	.	.	not appearance oriented
adventurous	.	.	.	.	.	cautious
aggressive	.	.	.	.	.	non-aggressive
competitive	.	.	.	.	.	non-competitive
easily hurt	.	.	.	.	.	not easily hurt
emotional	.	.	.	.	.	unemotional
excitable	.	.	.	.	.	not excitable
follower	.	.	.	.	.	leader
independent	.	.	.	.	.	dependent
objective	.	.	.	.	.	subjective
submissive	.	.	.	.	.	dominant

ASSIGNMENTS ▷ ▷ ▷ ▷ ▷ ▷ ▷ ▷

1 Mark your place on a scale 1 to 5 by each word on the chart. The number 1 indicates least like the quality and 5 indicates most like the quality.

(a) Ask a friend to consider your opinion of yourself.

(b) Circle the features you would most like to change.

(c) Discuss how a person could help her- or himself if the person is cautious but wants to be more adventurous, and so on through the list.

2 Identify the response in the two assignments on page 12 as

- aggressive **or**
- passive **or**
- assertive.

3 Now role-play the following situations in pairs, trying out the three different responses in assignment 2 above.

(a) You've lost your ticket on a train/bus journey and you need to persuade an official that you have paid.

(b) A classmate wants you to try drugs.

(c) Your girl/boyfriend tells you his parents are away and invites you to stay the night. You don't want to.

(d) Your parent/guardian says you have been on the phone too long.

(e) Your friend asks you what you think of his/her new hairstyle. You hate it.

(f) Think of some situations applicable to yourself.

WHAT'S SUCCESS?

Have you ever had one of those days when everything seems to go wrong, or right for that matter? Success is relative; to other people, other achievements, and to the effort put in. This is reflected in the following example.

The least successful animal rescue

The fireman's strike of 1978 made possible one of the great animal rescue attempts of all time. Valiantly, the British Army had taken over emergency firefighting and on 14 January they were called out by an elderly lady in South London to retrieve her cat which had become trapped up a tree. They arrived with impressive haste and soon discharged their duty. So grateful was the lady that she invited them all in for tea. Driving off later, with fond farewells completed, they ran over the cat and killed it.

From Stephen Pile, *The Book of Heroic Failures*, Viking, 1989

ASSIGNMENTS ▷ ▷ ▷ ▷ ▷ ▷ ▷ ▷

Discuss each of these issues in your group.

1 Is it better to try your best or to achieve results? Which is the real success?

2 Should school/college reports assess students more for their effort or for their achievement? Do you think this should change at all when you reach the sixth form?

3 How do you assess the success of your teachers in teaching you?

4 What is the most unsuccessful thing you have done? How might you have avoided failure on that occasion?

ASSIGNMENTS ▷ ▷ ▷ ▷ ▷ ▷ ▷ ▷

1 Look at the article opposite. What sort of sacrifices would you have had to make, and be making now, to have become a champion tennis player? At what age do you think that a person can decide if such sacrifices are worthwhile?

2 Make a list of what you consider to have been your three greatest successes ever? To what extent were these the reward for your effort? To what extent do you associate them with being happy, at the time and then subsequently?

3 'To travel hopefully is a better thing than to arrive, and the true success is to labour' (Robert Louis Stevenson writing in *El Dorado*). Choose four of your group to act as principals to debate for and against this motion. Other members of the group should make their own contribution to the discussion.

The price of success

John McEnroe is in love and the whole tennis world is aflutter. If twang go the strings of his heart, whence the strings of his racket? Those racket strings have been making such a special sound these past eight years that any change of tone or key could end up with the Grand Prix circuit being led by a different conductor.

Remember Maestro Borg? It was boredom that finished Bjorn – love came later. But if it is much too early to start thinking in terms of retirement as far as 26-year-old McEnroe is concerned, the emotional changes he has undergone during the past eight months have begun to have a noticeable effect on his tennis – not in the way he plays, but in how often.

For years I've heard John muttering, 'I must cut down. I've got to re-organise my schedule. This is crazy, man.' He would say that in Melbourne one week, Bucharest the next and, after repeating it to his father on his way through New York, would be saying it again three days later in Tokyo. Now, suddenly, he has found a reason to stop muttering and do something about it. Her name, just in case you have spent much of the year in Outer Mongolia, is Tatum O'Neal, child prodigy, child actress and Ryan's daughter. She is still very much the daughter, probably still an actress, although lacking in what McEnroe would call match practice, but at 21, has long since given up being a child.

Now, of course, McEnroe and Tatum have their own house, and, with the beach and the surf beckoning, it is hardly surprising John finds a Hilton hotel room with photographers camped outside – which would have been his lot had he played in Rotterdam as scheduled last March – a poor substitute for watching the sun set over the Pacific with his beloved one.

It is, of course, understandable that the superficial McEnroe watchers would regard him as the epitome of the spoilt, immature brat. But if his antics on court, his pouting, petulant refusal to accept authority and his uncontrollable fits of rage offer plenty of ammunition to fuel the charge, allow me to redress the balance. Evidence to the contrary is available.

I remember when he was asked by a parent what advice he had for those with children who were showing an exceptional aptitude for tennis. 'Don't force them to play all the time,' McEnroe answered. 'Encourage them to play other sports as well. Above all, let them have as normal a childhood as possible. Those growing up years are precious.' How immature is that?

The question now seems to be whether McEnroe can keep total cynicism at bay and sustain the private beliefs he has always held dear. He still loves tennis, but it is possible his appetite for the struggle he has to go through to air his exceptional gifts on the public stage may be on the wane. Maybe Tatum can help him, maybe not. In the meantime, we will have to wait and see whether the day is approaching that McEnroe spoke about when I asked him a couple of years ago when he was going to stop being upset about bad line calls. He shrugged and said, 'When it doesn't matter any more, I guess.' For the sake of all of us who like to hear those strings make that music, I hope it continues to matter for a little while yet. □

From Richard Evans in *Options*, July 1985

WHAT'S SUCCESS?

Complexities hold a real fascination

The myth that a long apprenticeship is required to learn to play real tennis was dispelled last weekend when Sally Jones, who took up the game seven months ago, won the United States women's open singles and doubles championships at Newport, Rhode Island.

Miss Jones has fine credentials for achieving excellence in the game. When at Oxford, where she read English, she represented the university against Cambridge at five sports: squash, tennis, netball, cricket and the modern pentathlon of running, riding, shooting, swimming and fencing. She hails from Coleshill in Warwickshire and represents the county at tennis; she was British schoolgirls' doubles champion at the age of 15.

Miss Jones is a popular personality in the Midlands, frequently in demand as a speaker to open fêtes and compere shows owing to her position as presenter with Central Television. She also works for ITN and TV a.m. as well as pursuing her profession as a journalist (she is a columnist for *Today*). Her writing has extended to five books: a children's story on tennis and others on West Country legends and folklore.

She owed her initiation into real tennis to an interview she conducted for *The Daily Express* with Lesley Ronaldson after she had narrowly failed to win the inaugural women's world championship in Melbourne last year. The principal appeal of the sport for Miss Jones lay in the subtlety and complexities of the game; she finds most other ball games by comparison 'childishly simple and repetitive'. She explains: 'The intellectual challenge posed by a game akin to three-dimensional chess means that once you're hooked on real tennis it is difficult to imagine playing anything else. There is a great physical thrill, too, when you really cut a ball properly to a good length.

'The fact that you can compete at a high level and still see yourself improving despite doing a very full-time job is an added attraction. The friendliness of the players is another delightful bonus. They all know each other and stay with one another at different tournaments around the world. There is none of the bitchiness and back-biting that you get at the big tennis tournaments. There is an awful lot of the amateur spirit which most other games have lost.'

From *The Times*, 22 May 1986

ASSIGNMENTS ▷ ▷ ▷ ▷ ▷ ▷ ▷ ▷

1 Make a list of Sally Jones's 'successes' as described here. Put these in the form of a curriculum vitae (see page 151).

2 What is the appeal of real tennis to Sally Jones?
How many of the same qualities apply to your enjoyment of whatever sport you do best?

3 What do you see as the main differences between Sally Jones and John McEnroe as sports persons?

Mom Is Outnumbered

By Barbara Roessner

HARTFORD, Connecticut – It was a typical scenario, woefully typical: two small boys who, from a distance, appeared to be engaged in the wholesome pursuit of examining shells they had gathered along the beach. I spied them from the window of our rented seaside cottage and was touched by this Norman Rockwell image, only to be jarred by an abrupt contortion of the happy idyll. Suddenly, rocks began to fly and shells began to shatter.

MEANWHILE

'What in hell are you guys doing?' I yelled from the window.

'We're wasting snails!' they exclaimed. On their faces I saw the flush and thrill of their act of destruction.

I had seen it many times before, and I have seen it many times since. I saw it recently on the countenance of a 3-year-old who spent the better part of an hour whipping the sharks in his closet with the sweet little jump rope the Easter Bunny brought him. I routinely see it in the eyes of his two older brothers as they examine their budding biceps in the bathroom mirror or plead with their father for one more showing of 'The Terminator'.

It is one of the many peculiarities that go with the territory I call home, a place overrun with male people. It is also one of the many reasons for this recurrent feeling I have that if I am to continue to be the sole female presence there, I will surely sink in a sea of testosterone.

It has become fashionable, after many years of denial, to recognize the profound differences between males and females. My personal recognition is nothing new, nor is it in any way an ideological or theoretical exercise. For some time I have been bombarded with overwhelming anecdotal evidence whose effect on me is purely visceral. It makes me want to scream, which I often do.

Perhaps the maleness of my surroundings strikes me as especially pungent because it is so unlike the surroundings of my youth. I grew up in a household dominated by females – six of us vs. two of them, counting both parents and offspring. My lone brother has long complained of being an oddity among his five sisters. Now I can sympathize.

My childhood home was an emotion-packed place. Occasionally my brother lured one of us into physical combat, but wars of sensitivity were far more common. Tears flowed frequently; blood rarely. Academic achievement was highly valued; there was no great premium placed on athletic prowess or a knowledge of automotive parts.

All in all, it must have been terribly frustrating for the minority. Almost as frustrating as it is for me to be forever bracing myself against the crashing of bodies, the perpetual vibration of walls and floors, the omnipresence of grimy space-eating sports equipment and, of course, the constant screeching of imaginary vehicles skidding out of control and into ear-splitting collisions.

If all of this affirms the time-worn stereotypes of male and female behaviour, if it offends those who would prefer to see the traditional sex roles confounded, I'm sorry. But I can't help it. I'm lonely. I want a friend. I want an ally.

In a month or so, a new member of the family is scheduled to arrive. On those rare occasions when I put aside my worries about the health and well-being of my pending offspring, I find myself longing for a child who will not stash motorcycle magazines under the bed at age 3, who might consider the possibility that 'I like your tires' isn't the only compliment one can pay a stranger.

I yearn for someone who, someday, might be inclined to shop at my side. And sometimes I lapse into fantasies of more immediate gratification, of tiny smocked dresses and patent leather shoes, of braids and barrettes. Oh God, sometimes I imagine a shelf full of dolls.

How can I put it? I'm dying for a girl.

The Hartford Courant

From the *International Herald Tribune*, 19 April 1988

ASSIGNMENTS ▷ ▷ ▷ ▷ ▷ ▷ ▷ ▷

1 On your own, jot down how you are affected by the obsessions of your brother(s) and/or sister(s).

2 To what extent do you influence them?

3 In groups of four, discuss whether you agree that there are 'profound differences between males and females'.

4 How might this parent have changed her sons' behaviour?

5 Does it matter? You could perhaps hold a debate on this topic.

GENDER AND ROLES

Are there still double standards?

'Britain is still an exceptionally misogynist society. I think the pressures on boys – of competitiveness, male bravado, contemptuousness of women – are very difficult to fight against.' Would you agree? Despite years of feminist activity, are women getting a 'fair deal' at work or play? This article looks into the playground and suggests that one of the problems for women is that they limit themselves too much. Women may have been socialised into certain roles in childhood, but they should learn that they can seek out and enjoy authority in all areas of their lives.

ASSIGNMENTS ▷ ▷ ▷ ▷ ▷ ▷ ▷ ▷

1 What is your reaction to the verbal sexual abuse described in the article 'She is a slag, he is a stud'? What does the writer mean by: 'To call her a bitch or a slag or an old bag can be just as harmful, and just as effective in controlling her'?

2 Why do girls not 'challenge the profound unfairness that underlies the abuse'? How should they do so?

GENDER AND ROLES

She is a slag, he is a stud

'IF YOU don't like them, they'll call you a tight bitch. If you go with them they'll call you a slag afterwards.'

It seems that the 'double standard' of morality between the sexes, after three decades of the women's liberation movement, persists and flourishes. The boys of this generation (as of most others) are free to brag about their sexual conquests, whether with truth or not. The girls, while arguably freer than before to be sexually active, are as anxious and possibly more vulnerable than ever.

. . . The denigration of a girl as a 'slag' (the word's meaning as 'prostitute' is dated from the 1950s) has . . . become an imperceptible, taken-for-granted part of a commonsense view of the world.

There are many other words – 'bitch,' 'cow,' 'dog,' 'slut' – which, like slag, are used all the time, by girls as well as by boys, spoken in many different moods, and applied to all kinds of girls, irrespective of their actual sexual availability or experience. The abusive words therefore appear to mean very little. But their lack of significance does not imply a lack of effect. . . .

The use of words has material implications. You can't make a distinction between hitting a woman and abusing her verbally. To call her a bitch or a slag or an old bag can be just as harmful, and just as effective in controlling her. . . .

Girls, under the pressure of having their sexuality always up for comment, do not see or challenge the profound unfairness that underlies the abuse; and they have no language (and perhaps no heart) to retaliate to it in kind. (There is no derogatory word for a sexually active boy – 'stud' has strong admiring overtones –

while there is no 'good' word for a sexually active girl.) . . .

Their oppression does not only come from the boys. Other girls reinforce this form of control on a girl: and not only on her sexuality, but on her behaviour, clothes, friendships, school work and social life, too.

The only way a girl can redeem a (however unjustly) lost reputation is by finding a steady boyfriend and thereby asserting that she is not sexually available to all. Her only acceptable entry into the adult world is, therefore, through a relationship with a boy.

From the *Observer*, 15 June 1986

IT'S NEVER TOO LATE

One of the normal requirements of the school or college sixth form is that you opt for subjects that will be in some way 'useful' to you in the future; for instance, if you want to go into one particular line of work, you probably have been advised to choose relevant subjects to study. But it can often be frustrating to feel that you are set on only one course of action. This unit lets you see if you can extend your horizons and interests or simply change some behaviour.

The following extract is taken from an introduction by Willy Russell to an edition of his play *Educating Rita*. Those of you who know the play or film will recognise similarities between the playwright and his character Rita.

Educating Willy Russell

At home there were conferences, discussions, rows and slanging matches all on the same subject – me and the job I'd get. Eventually my mother resolved it all. She suggested I become a ladies' hairdresser! I can only think that a desire to have her hair done free must have clouded her normally reasonable mind. It was such a bizzare suggestion that I went along with it. I went to a college for a year or so and pretended to learn all about hairdressing. In reality most of my time was spent at parties or arranging parties. It was a good year but when it ended I had to go to work. Someone was actually prepared to hire me as a hairdresser, to let me loose on the heads of innocent and unsuspecting customers. There were heads scalded during shampooing, heads which should have become blonde but turned out green, heads of Afro frizz (before Afro frizz had been invented) and heads rendered temporarily bald. Somehow, probably from moving from one shop to another before my legendary abilities were known, I survived. For six years I did a job I didn't understand and didn't like. Eventually I even had my own small salon and it was there that on slack days I would retire to the back room and try to do the one and only thing I felt I understood, felt that I could do: write.

I wrote songs mostly but tried, as well, to write sketches and poetry, even a book. But I kept getting interrupted by women who, reasonably enough on their part, wanted their hair done. It dawned upon me that if ever I was to become a writer I had first to get myself into the sort of world which allowed for, possibly even encouraged such aspiration. But that would mean a drastic change of course. Could I do it? Could I do something which those around me didn't understand? I would have to break away. People would be puzzled and hurt. I compromised. I sensed that the world in which I would be able to write would be the academic world. Students have long holidays. I'd be able to spend a good part of the year writing and the other part learning to do a job, teaching perhaps, which would pay the rent. I wasn't qualified to train as a teacher but I decided to dip my toe in the water and test the temperature. I enrolled in a night class for O level English Literature and passed it. To go to a college though, I'd need at least five O levels. Taking them at night school would take too long. I had to find a college which would let me take a full-time course, pack everything into one year. I found a college but no authority was prepared to give me a maintenance grant or even pay my fees. I knew I couldn't let the course go, knew I could survive from day to day – but how was I going to find the money to pay the fees? The hairdressing paid nothing worth talking of.

I heard of a job, a contract job in Fords, cleaning oil from the girders high above the machinery. With no safety equipment whatsoever and with oil on every girder the danger was obvious. But the money was big.

I packed up the hairdresser's and joined the night-shift girder cleaners. Some of them fell and were injured, some of them took one look at the job and walked away. Eventually there were just a few of us desperate or daft enough to take a chance.

I stayed in that factory just long enough to earn the fees I needed; no extras, nothing. Once I'd earned enough for the fees, I came down from the girders, collected my money and walked away. I enrolled at the college and one day in September made my way along the stone-walled drive. The obvious difference in age between me and the sixteen-year-olds pouring down the drive made me feel exposed and nervous but as I entered the glass doors of Childwall College I felt as if I'd made it back to the beginning. I could start again. I felt at home.

From Willy Russell, *Educating Rita*, Longman Study Texts, Longman, 1985

ASSIGNMENTS ▷ ▷ ▷ ▷ ▷ ▷ ▷ ▷

1 What sort of person do you think Willy Russell was when he left school? How did he change?

2 Write down the steps he took in deciding to become a writer.

3 Ask a friend to write a brief description of you as you are now, and as she or he imagines you will be in five years' time. How do you feel about these viewpoints?

4 Now ask the same friend (if you are still talking to each other) to tell you honestly one characteristic piece of behaviour of yours that she or he would recommend changing. Will you try?

5 If you have made a wrong decision about your subjects, how can you change this?

6 Think about something you would like to do in the next year and write down the steps you would need to take to achieve this.

AN ADULT IN SOCIETY

Like it or not, you are a member of a society made up of a lot of different people. What will be your attitudes to those other people and to society in general? How do you see your place in society and how much does it allow you to change the way society behaves, for better for worse?

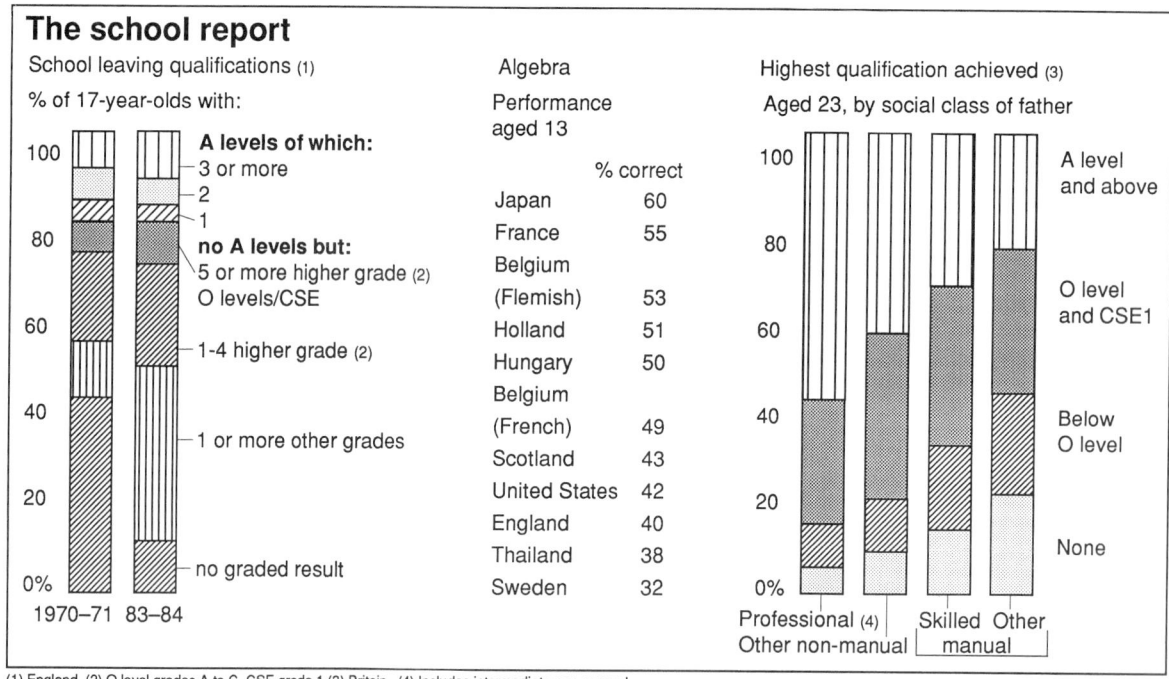

The school report

School leaving qualifications (1)

% of 17-year-olds with:

A levels of which:
- 3 or more
- 2
- 1

no A levels but:
- 5 or more higher grade (2) O levels/CSE
- 1-4 higher grade (2)
- 1 or more other grades
- no graded result

1970–71 83–84

Algebra

Performance aged 13

	% correct
Japan	60
France	55
Belgium (Flemish)	53
Holland	51
Hungary	50
Belgium (French)	49
Scotland	43
United States	42
England	40
Thailand	38
Sweden	32

Highest qualification achieved (3)

Aged 23, by social class of father

- A level and above
- O level and CSE1
- Below O level
- None

Professional (4) | Skilled Other
Other non-manual | manual

(1) England (2) O level grades A to C, CSE grade 1 (3) Britain (4) Includes intermediate non-manual
Sources DES, The second IEA mathematics, RA Garden, National Child Development Study

From *The Economist*, 15 March 1989

ASSIGNMENTS ▷ ▷ ▷ ▷ ▷ ▷ ▷ ▷

1 From the data, find what proportion of your age group share the same qualifications as you expect to achieve on leaving school. Do you feel that your qualifications will place you in a better or worse position in society? Say why.

2 How have school leaving qualifications changed in general from the 1970s to the 1980s? Do these changes suggest that

schools are preparing people well for society or not? What else would you wish to know to help you decide your answer?

3 What is the connection, in general terms, between social class and educational qualifications? Why might this connection exist? Do you agree that education can and should change society, or not?

AN ADULT IN SOCIETY

Manny Shinwell on 'Behaviour'

*Manny Shinwell was a left-wing politician
who was born in a Glasgow slum in the
nineteenth century. He served as a cabinet
minister in the twentieth century and died in
1986 as a member of the House of Lords.*

What has worried me for many years has been the deterioration of both
personal and social behaviour. Going back to the beginning of the century,
when I entered public life, although social conditions were far from satisfactory
– vast unemployment, most of it unregistered, no social security, thousands of
people actually starving, maternal mortality rates very high . . . since then
there has undoubtedly been a deterioration in manners. There is a lack of
consideration for other people. We're pushing each other around far more
aggressively than when I was younger. [Then] if one went on a tram and it
was crowded, one would always make way for one of the female sex,
particularly if the person was somewhat older – sometimes because she was
much younger! And the behaviour of those looking after passengers,
collectors and so on – they were without question better behaved and more
considerate than those now on the buses.

'To what do you attribute this deterioration primarily?'

There are all sorts of reasons for it. In those days – although, as I've said,
there was excessive poverty and far more ill-health – somehow people didn't
push each other around so much. They did have consideration. If you walked
along a street and met someone, the first thing they would ask was, 'Are you
working?' I remember that so well. It wasn't, 'Are you keeping well?' It was,
'Are you working?' Because there was so much unemployment. People had
concern. There was more neighbourliness amongst the working class than
there is now. You always talked over the garden fence [*a telling criticism of
municipal high-rise flats*] or stood at the gate. And women would congregate,
especially on washing-days. The water supply was centralised – stand-pipes –
not every house had water piped in. People met, enquired about each other.
Certainly amongst children, manners were – I wouldn't say impeccable – but
far better than nowadays, when children don't seem to care two hoots for
their elders.

   To me, looking at the world as it is – as a person who's been a long time
in politics – you ask yourself, 'What's gone wrong?' Is it politics have gone
wrong? Isn't it BEHAVIOUR?

   Take South Africa. Take Russia. It's a matter of behaviour – by which I
mean consideration, to some extent compassion – behaviour. How one
conducts oneself. I apply that [criterion] to the coloured people. I have no
prejudice against coloured people – none at all – except when a coloured

AN ADULT IN SOCIETY

man becomes aggressive. I have the same feelings with a white man. It's a question of education – and yet you can have the best education in the world and your behaviour can be abominable.

I would go so far as to say – and you may think this an exaggeration – that looking at the world as it is today, the one thing we need above all else is BETTER BEHAVIOUR.

From John Doxat, *Shinwell Talking*, Quiller Press, 1984

ASSIGNMENTS ▷ ▷ ▷ ▷ ▷ ▷ ▷ ▷

1 Do you believe that social behaviour has worsened? Do your parents/guardians tell you the same thing, or are there some ways in which behaviour has improved?

2 Do you give up your seat, ask how other people are, or curse at other people? Do you see these as aspects of good or bad behaviour? Do you agree that issues in national and international politics may reflect similar 'matters of behaviour'?

3 To what extent do you agree that the following social changes have affected the behaviour of modern society:
   • local environment and planning?
   • working married women?
   • education?

To what extent does the colour of your skin determine your identity? To what extent do your physical characteristics determine the response of others? What part does your ethnic and cultural background play in forming your personality? And how significant to your self-image is the in-put of your family? At the end of this unit, you may like to discuss these questions. The first part of the unit deals with the issue of identity by focusing on black children in white families. The assignments are on page 26.

The case of Mary

Mary came into care under the voluntary section of the Children's Act. Mother was black, single and lived in a damp council flat, had lost her job and was receiving social work help. She agreed for her child to come into care for a short while until her problems were resolved. At times she used to become depressed but maternal grandmother would help. When the social worker became involved she formed the opinion that Mary was caught between biological mother and maternal grandmother. Mary was placed with a white family in a rural area. The local authority terminated access on the following grounds:

a) The department had been unhappy about the nature of mother's visit to the foster home and the effect that her contact had on Mary.

b) There was little or no early bonding between Mary and mother. Mary's mother was not a real parent in the emotional sense.

c) Mary had reacted and was reacting badly to visits from mother: crying, inability to sleep, lack of concentration.

d) Presents from mother have on many occasions seemed inappropriate.

e) Mother had little conception of the enormity of the step for Mary if she were to move back to her mother in that area. Mary had spent only a small part of her life in the 'black' community: to return her to mother would be to return her to an alien environment to the care of virtual strangers.

f) Mary wished to remain with her foster parents.

At age 2 the child was observed to be showing signs of 'identity confusion': a) scratching off her skin, b) had an aversion to black people.

From John W. Small (Director, New Black Families), *The Crisis in Adoption*

COLOUR

1 There has been a decrease in the number of children, especially white, available for adoption? Why is this?

2 What do you think are the characteristics of white couples who have wanted specifically to adopt black children?

3 Is it better for a child to be placed 'transracially' than to have no family upbringing at all?

4 Give actual examples of ways in which adoptive white parents can enhance positive black identity in their black children.

5 Should children of 'mixed race parentage' call themselves black?

6 Make a list of ways any family can make their children racially aware.

7 Role-play a case conference of social workers with different points of view about how best to help Mary. You might need to find out how a 'case conference' runs, first.

1 Go through the article opposite and jot down the different scenes. In groups of three or four, take a scene each to role-play. Try out different endings, for example, Geoff Small overhearing the club bouncer let Tim Marshall in; Tim coming back with Geoff after he had 'joined' the snooker club. Demonstrate one of your role-plays to the whole group.

2 Put a volunteer as Geoff Small and another as Tim Marshall into a 'hot seat'. The rest of the group ask questions of each character about their experiences. (The volunteers do not have to be the same colour or sex as the originals, but they should try to 'get into their skins' for this activity.)
Afterwards talk to the volunteers about how they felt role-playing the two men. Do you think women would be treated the same way?

3 Hold a group discussion on ways of implementing the statement Tim Marshall makes: 'After this I'd like to think that if someone makes a racist remark, I would not let it ride ... this has shown me a different way of leading my life.'

All those little white lies . . .

The progress of
two men through
our prejudiced
society is observed
by **Brian James**

On BBC1 tonight television begins an 'investigation' made no less compelling by the leaden feeling from the first minute that we know precisely what they will discover: a mirror held up to British society reflects back little that is very new, and absolutely nothing that is very nice.

The subject is racial prejudice, and the method taken by the *Brass Tacks* team was to send two young men, one black (Geoff Small) one white (Tim Marshall) to Bristol to make identical applications for somewhere to live, for jobs, for admission to pubs, and then compare their experiences.

Small, aged 26, bright enough to go through grammar school and earn two degrees, and Marshall, aged 28, who did six years in the RAF before becoming a radio reporter, began proving their case the moment they started seeking a room.

We follow them – always first the black Geoff, then 15 minutes later the white Tim – to meet landladies. 'A room? Sorry, love, nothing at the moment,' two of the first three tell Small. Both have a bed for Marshall. In this first programme, of 15 bed-and-breakfast establishments, one third treat the white more favourably (in terms of price if not availability) than the black.

Afterwards the two men discuss this first finding. Small: 'I

By colour divided: Geoff Small and Tim Marshall, who hold up a mirror to the painful truth about racial attitudes in Britain

don't understand it, but then I don't see why I don't understand it. Yes, I am hurt. A bit shocked. Yet if you are black, this is part of your life.' What appears to reach him is that those who have often been the most friendly are the most deceitful.

Next they try for flats, telephoning in answer to newspaper adverts. Of 16 landlords who respond with, 'Yes, it's still free, call round', three react to the first sight of Small's colour with a glib, 'Sorry, it's gone'. Others say they have more to interview, they'll let him know.

An awful thing is the way they then involve Tim Marshall in what he calls their 'whites-only club'. 'Had a coloured chap before you,' one tells him. 'Not suitable at all. What I want is a decent, honest sort of chap.' Small has heard this stolen fragment of interview a score of times; yet in the preview theatre, his face still tightens. Another rejecting landlord, uneasy perhaps, gives his justification: 'Nothing against them . . . seemed a nice chap . . . but a big

chap, bit of a handful . . . a bit arrogant . . . if there was a problem . . .'

Small and Marshall go out for entertainment. 'Sorry,' two bouncers tell Geoff, 'couples only'. Ten minutes later the unaccompanied Marshall is greeted with: 'Evening sir, come in . . . two pounds please'. Small seems unsurprised that at this club, and the next, a rejecting bouncer is also black. 'Uh . . . the guy might need the job.'

They try for jobs. First, evening work in a public house. Again, the job has gone when Small applies to a friendly barmaid, but mysteriously reappears when Marshall calls minutes later. 'The landlord did say it was a rough sort of pub,' Marshall says, surely well aware that it is places like this that social theory and street life have an uneasy and potentially violent interface. 'Perhaps he was just trying to save you grief.' 'Nah,' Small says. As he is to make clear later, he wants neither sympathy nor explanation from whites; just 'my share of the pie'.

AN ADULT IN THE FAMILY

Do you like living at home? Or do you long to set up a place of your own? Your answers to these questions may depend on how you get on with your family. Let's look at family life, your position as you become an adult, and some of the problems and benefits of group living.

Imagine that you and your family go out in your family car to see a family film before going home to your family house for a family meal in front of the TV. Certainly if you watch the advertisements on your TV you may feel that people live, spend and enjoy family living all the time. But do such families exist? Does yours fit the advertiser's dream: Two parents with 1.64 children and a dog? Probably not. Family life has changed since this image was created, or perhaps it never was like that at all.

The tables below show the statistical picture of family life in Great Britain and compare the 1980s with the 1970s and 1960s. It seems that less than half of all the people now live in families made up of two parents and their children. Look at the data more carefully now to see how things have changed, and how your own family situation fits in with the general picture.

People in households 1

Great Britain — Percentage

- Other households — 100
- Lone parent with dependent children 2
- Married couple with independent children only — 75
- Married couple with dependent children 2 — 50
- Married couple, no children — 25
- Living alone — 0

1961 1971 1981 1983

1 The data for 1961, 1971, and 1981 are taken from the Population Censuses for those years; the 1983 data are from the General Household Survey.
2 These family types may also include independent children.

People who live alone 1

Great Britain	Percentage	
	1973	1983
Percentage of people aged:		
16-24	0.5	0.9
25-44	2.4	4.2
45-64	8.1	9.3
65-74	25.7	27.6
75 or over	40.0	46.6
All aged 16 or over	6.7	8.7
Percentage of males aged:		
65-74	13.1	15.3
75 or over	24.2	28.4
Percentage of females aged:		
65-74	35.8	36.8
75 or over	48.0	56.8

1 Private households only

Source: General Household Survey 1973 and 1983

AN ADULT IN THE FAMILY

ASSIGNMENTS ▷ ▷ ▷ ▷ ▷ ▷ ▷ ▷

1 According to the figures, what has been the change in the proportion of households with dependent children?

2 Do you think of yourself as a dependent or independent member of your family? See if you can give reasons for your answer.

3 Why do you think there has been a fall in the proportion of the population that lives in 'married couple' families?

4 Why do you think there are more people living alone? Use the figures to help you answer this.

5 Why are teenagers reluctant to stay at home in the evenings?

6 What do you recommend for an enjoyable family evening?

7 How do you think parents feel when their children leave home?

8 What will be the good things you will remember about living with your family?

9 What tasks are performed equally with the adults in your household? Compare with others in your group and discuss the significance of the general results.

LIVING WITH PARENTS

For most people the very first relationship they form is with an adult in the family into which they are born or placed. Traditionally this relationship is with the mother or father figure. With luck – and much hard work – this relationship will be a lasting one, a special one for both parties. During a child's teenage years, however, this relationship will be put to many tests, as it develops from one of dependence to one, ideally, of friendship.

Already more than a million children live with a step-parent. At least a further one and a half million are growing up with a divorced or separated parent who may re-marry. The introduction of a new adult into the family can put huge strain on all its members.

Parenting is probably one of the most difficult roles anyone plays. We should learn from our parents' mistakes, but, in fact, research has shown the opposite: that we repeat the patterns set by our parents all too easily. We are also all affected by the 'experts' of our day, and the upbringing children receive may well be influenced by strong outside opinion about what is 'right' and 'wrong' at the time.

This unit gives you the chance to consider some patterns of parenting, to criticise and laugh at them, and then maybe to move to a new understanding of the way you would like to bring up children yourself.

ASSIGNMENTS ▷ ▷ ▷ ▷ ▷ ▷ ▷ ▷

1 Would you be embarrassed to have your parents/guardians with you in the following situations:
   • going shopping?
   • going to a place of worship?
   • being collected by them from a party?
   Is there any occasion when you have been really embarrassed by your parents?

2 How do you think parents feel in the above situations? What is the most embarrassing thing you have ever done to them?

3 Describe three situations in which you would be really pleased to have your parents/guardians with you.

THE PITFALLS AND HOW TO AVOID THEM

Before becoming a step-parent:

- Discuss with your partner the basics of bringing up children. Do you agree on bedtime, TV, responsibilities, schooling, punishment?

- Get to know the children before marriage.

- Practise spending time as a 'family' – perhaps taking a short holiday together.

- Agree on the practicalities – where to live, finances, whether the wife will work or not, having more children, choosing names.

Once you are a step-parent:

- Agree on explicit house-rules.

- Try to find time, no matter how short, to talk as a family.

- Remember that clashes are common in all families: they just tend to be more intense in step-families.

- The National Step-family Association has been set up to help all members of step-families. You can reach a local group through the head office at Room 3, Ross Street Community Centre, Ross Street, Cambridge CB1 3BS (0223 356322).

From *The Times*, 27 June 1986

LIVING WITH PARENTS

A son must . . .

A son should respect his father
He should not have to be taught to respect his father
It is something that is natural
That's how I've brought up my son anyway.

Of course a father must be worthy of respect
He can forfeit a son's respect
But I hope at least that my son will respect me, if
only for leaving him free to respect me or not.

R. D. Laing

Do a Dance for Daddy

Do a dance for Daddy, make your Daddy smile
Be his little angel
Remember you're on trial
Mummy's competition, Mummy brings you down
When you're up there shining
She always wears a frown

Do a dance for Daddy. Bend and dip and whirl
You've got all that talent
'Cause you're Daddy's girl
Daddy is your hero, witty and superb
With a sign upon his door
That reads 'Do not disturb'

Look your best for Daddy
Pass your test for Daddy
Stand up tall for Daddy
Do it all for Daddy

Some day when you're older you will find romance
Someone just like Daddy
Will whistle and you'll dance
You'll recall that music when you're on the shelf
You danced for all the Daddies
But you never found yourself

Paint your eyes for Daddy
Win a prize for Daddy
Swim to France for Daddy
Do your dance for Daddy

Fran Landesman

LIVING WITH PARENTS

Laura faces hostility

Laura was 34 when she married a divorced man with a daughter of 12 and a son of 10. Laura had been a friend of the children's mother and had known them since they were six and eight. She says: 'Although I had nothing at all to do with the break-up of their parents' marriage, both children were extremely hostile to me after I married their father. And meeting such implacable hostility head-on was a bit of a shock.

My step-daughter, for instance, would come into the room to talk to her father and completely ignore me. Yet this was a child I had read stories to, taken out for treats. She just found it extremely difficult adjusting to the idea of me as a step-mother rather than a friend of her mother. This is still a problem, even though her father and I have a cordial relationship with her mother and the man she is living with.'

Laura admits that things improved slightly when her son, now three, was born. 'He has forged a link between me and my step-daughter: she is devoted to him. But as she has become less hostile, my step-son has become more so. He feels ambivalent about my son. He likes him, but he sees him as a rival too. He's taken away the special place he had, both as the youngest and as the only son.'

From *The Times*, 27 June 1986

ASSIGNMENTS ▷ ▷ ▷ ▷ ▷ ▷ ▷ ▷

1 The shorter poem opposite comes from R. D. Laing's volume called *Knots*. First try to untangle its meaning.

2 Does R. D. Laing's poem represent a typical 'pattern of parenting' today? What do you think of it? Would you change it? If so how?

3 Apply the same questions to Fran Landesman's 'cameo'.

4 The two poems look at relationships that typically exist with the father-figure. How true are they of relationships with mothers?

5 Look at the article on page 31 again. Draw up lists of 'pitfalls and how to avoid them' entitled 'Before becoming – and once you are – a step-child'.

6 How many of the suggestions in the extract and your lists could be applied to improve family living generally? *And* how would you, in the child-role, attempt to implement them?

7 Now consider the 'case study' of Laura and her new family. Either write the letter the step-daughter or son might have written to an agony aunt – and the reply she or he might have received, or role-play a conversation between one of the children and an adult asked for advice.

LOVE RULES

Regulating sexual practices?

'But I love him . . .', 'You would if you really loved me . . .!' How often does the word 'love' get abused? Frequently it is used as a cover-up for lust.

● ●

American Magazine once ran a monthly column in which readers would send in unusual laws that their states, cities, or townships had promulgated. The columns included such legal oddities as the following:

In Iowa a kiss lasting more than five minutes is against the law.

Firemen in Huntington, West Virginia may not whistle or flirt with any woman passing a firehouse.

Serenading your girlfriend is illegal in Kalamazoo, Michigan.

It is illegal to ogle women from a public vehicle in Detroit, Michigan.

In Miami, Florida, it is against the law to molest an alligator.

A man may not give his sweetheart a box of candy weighing less than 50 lbs in Burley, Idaho.

It is illegal in Indianapolis, Indiana for a moustached man to kiss anybody.

Making love in the front seat of a taxicab during working hours is prohibited by law in Springfield, Massachusetts.

No one may sit closer than eight inches to a person of the opposite sex on Connecticut park benches.

Atlanta, Georgia has a city ordinance that prohibits 'unseemly displays of affection'.

Kissing in the moonlight without a chaperone is strictly forbidden in Silver Lane, Connecticut.

In Norton, Virginia, it is against the law to tickle a young girl.

Residents of Tulsa, Oklahoma are forbidden to kiss in public.

As ridiculous as these laws may seem, they are actual laws in effect somewhere in the United States. Although it is doubtful that they are rigidly enforced, these laws represent some of the ways in which this society has tried to regulate the sexual practices of its members.

From *Go To Health*, Dell Publishing, NY

● ●

LOVE RULES

Taboo Zones

A Taboo Zone is an area of the body which a companion may not touch.
Each of us has a sense of body-privacy, but the strength of this varies from
person to person, culture to culture, and relationship to relationship. Above
all, it varies according to the part of our body which is experiencing physical
contact. If a companion touches a 'public zone', such as the hand, then no
problem arises; but if the same companion reaches out to make contact with
a 'private zone', such as the genitals, then the result can be anything from
embarrassment to anger. Only lovers and parents with babies have
completely free access to all parts of the body. For everyone else there is a
graded scale of body-contact taboos.

A careful study was made recently of the Taboo Zones of college graduates
in the United States. Their body-surfaces were divided up into twelve
contact-zones and then they were asked how likely they were to be touched
in these different areas by: (1) their mothers; (2) their fathers; (3) friends of
the same sex; and (4) friends of the opposite sex. Four degrees of
touch-table were allowed for: touched frequently, touched moderately, touched
rarely and touched hardly ever or never.

What emerges from these differences is that each relationship has its own
unique combination of 'go' and 'no-go' areas.

From D. Morris, *Manwatching*, Jonathan Cape, 1978

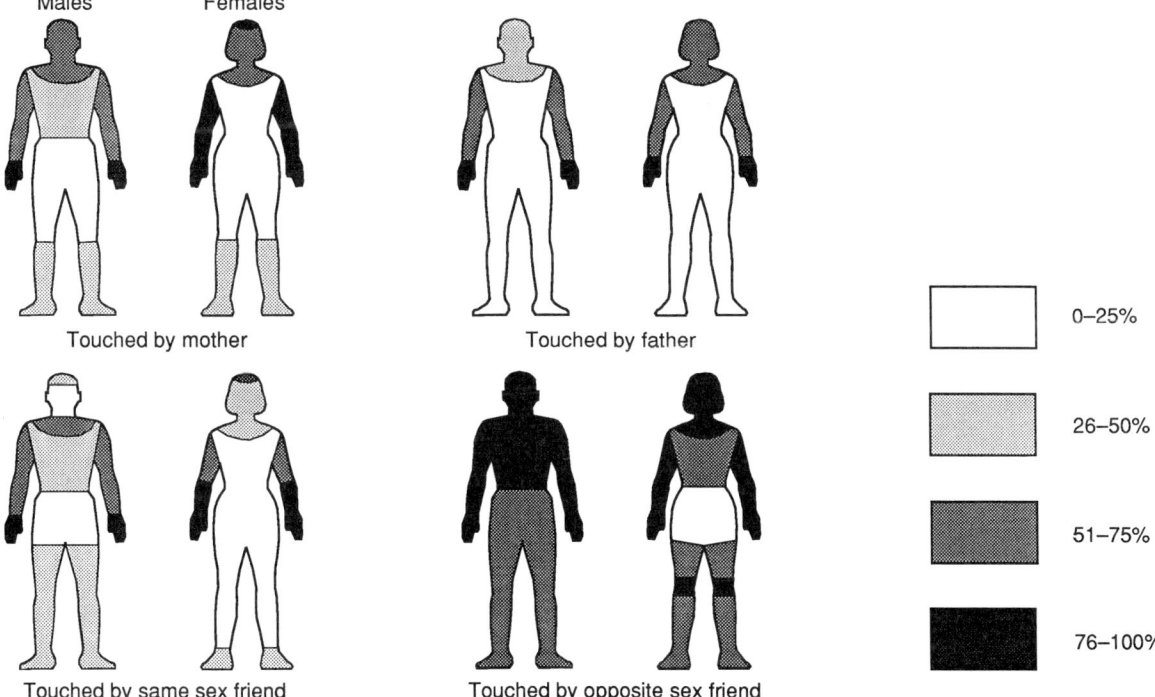

Males   Females

Touched by mother

Touched by father

Touched by same sex friend

Touched by opposite sex friend

0–25%

26–50%

51–75%

76–100%

LOVE RULES

ASSIGNMENTS ▷ ▷ ▷ ▷ ▷ ▷ ▷ ▷

1 Use the drawings in the extract from Desmond Morris's book *Manwatching* (page 35) to assess the typical areas of the body that 'receive attention' from different groups of people. Why do you think men reject caresses to the upper part of the body from anyone other than a girlfriend? Why too, is the male pubic area less of a taboo area to a girlfriend than hers is to a boyfriend?

2 How to deal with violation of the 'private zones' is a subject under close scrutiny now. In a group, discuss the words you would use to prevent someone you know from touching you in 'no-go' areas. These people will include boy/girl friends with whom you do not wish (yet?) to have a sexual relationship and adults, perhaps in the family, seeking sexual gratification. You might like to make a poster to display in the school to help others.

3 Read through the crazy laws that exist, but presumably are not enforced, in the United States (page 34). What laws exist in this country to regulate sexual practices? What do you think of them?

4 Recently an MP tried, unsuccessfully, to introduce a law prohibiting nude pictures in newspapers. Her argument was that it encouraged sexual assaults. What do you think of this viewpoint?

5 How can innocent people be best protected from sexual assault?

WHAT'S IN A MARRIAGE?

Marriage still seems to be one of the foundations on which our society is based. Despite attempts at varying the patterns of social living, people are still pairing off, and often getting married. It is very likely that if you marry it will be to someone similar to yourself in terms of background, age, and income, and also in terms of shared interests and ambitions. This may be because you met in a situation – like a club or on a course – which was mutually acceptable. But it may also be as a result of unconscious attraction, which you may only discover later, but at the time no doubt thought was 'chemistry'.

ASSIGNMENTS ▷ ▷ ▷ ▷ ▷ ▷ ▷ ▷

1 Try the exercise described by the family therapist in conversation with John Cleese. Concentrate only on 'the feeling' you receive about the person, not what you already know. What patterns emerge?

2 Think about and write down points on backgrounds, histories and attitudes of the adults in your family. For instance what is their placing (first born, second and so on) in their own families? Were there similar patterns in their two families or did they suffer in some way when they were a similar age? What do you think brought them together?

• •

Families and how to survive them

John What's the exercise for?

Robin Its purpose is to show what lies behind the way that couples pick each other out across a crowded room! And it demonstrated to me more clearly than I'd ever realised how unconscious attractions work, and what they're about.

John You mean it shows how we pick each other without knowing anything about each other?

Robin Yes. The trainees do this exercise very early on – in fact ideally when they're still complete strangers. They're put together in a group and asked to choose another person from the group who either makes them think of someone in their family or, alternatively, gives them the feeling that they would have filled a 'gap' in their family. And – here's the interesting bit – they're not allowed to speak at all while they're choosing. They just stand up and wander around looking at all the others. When they've all chosen someone, that is when they're in pairs, they are told to talk together for a time, to see if they can find out what made them pick each other. They're encouraged to compare their family backgrounds. Next, each couple is asked to choose another couple, in order to make foursomes. And then, each foursome is asked to form itself into a family of some kind, agreeing with each other what role in the family each person will take. Then they talk together about what it was in their family backgrounds that led to their decisions. And finally, they report to the group what they've discovered.

From Robin Skynner and John Cleese, *Families and How to Survive Them*, Methuen Paperback, 1984

• •

WHAT'S IN A MARRIAGE?

'Married people look dull and bored'

One of the criticisms people make about marriage is that it must get boring after a while. This is what one couple told a newspaper:

> **'You can always spot married people because, mainly, they look so dull and bored. So John and I sat down and thought up all the typically boring things married people seem to do. Then we made a list so we don't do the same.'**
>
> ROSA

● ●

The long list of rules was:

His	*Hers*
1. No pipe and slippers	1. No rollers
2. No gardening	2. No gossiping
3. No local	3. No dressing-gowns
4. No tinkering with the car	4. No women's magazines
5. No dog	5. No tinned foods
6. No reading newspapers at breakfast	6. No coffee mornings
7. No sleeping in armchair	7. No membership of women's groups
8. No talking about work	8. No washing machine
9. No excuses to have a night out with the boys	9. No ornaments about the house
10. No wearing old cardigans	10. No nagging
11. No short back and sides	11. No HP agreements

His and Hers

1. No house with a mortgage   2. No children for five years

● ●

From 'The Bride and Groom Plan a Happy Unmarriage', *Daily Mirror*, 1970 in Carol Adams and Rae Lawi Kietis, *The Gender Trap*, Virago, 1976

ASSIGNMENTS ▷ ▷ ▷ ▷ ▷ ▷ ▷ ▷

1 Consider the lists of things to avoid for marriage to be happy, written in 1970. What's your opinion of these rules today?

2 Now make a list that aims to make a marriage happy. Is such a list a good idea?

WHAT'S IN A MARRIAGE?

The institution of marriage

The following article may seem surprising to some of you, suggesting, as it does, that marriage is still a desirable institution.

Marriage 'still firmly rooted'

A major survey by the Marriage Research Council shows most of those who marry do so because it confers adulthood and status, and gives a purpose to lives and work.

Some of those questioned said they were glad to lay down the burden of 'freedom' which went with a single life.

But the researchers say there is real conflict, once the knot has been tied, between reality and the romantic ideal of a perfect relationship.

In the first investigation of its kind in Britain, 65 couples were followed through the first six years of married life.

The couples all married in 1979 and were interviewed three months later. They were questioned again six years later.

What surprised the sociologists was the abiding strength of marriage as an institution, and the willingness with which people took on the 'shackles' of domestic life.

The couples gave reasons for marriage which showed the institution to be just as important as it was when their parents married. Few said they married because they had found the perfect relationship.

It was confusion between importance of marriage and expectations of relationships that raised problems.

'People went into marriage because they believed in the institution. But in the course of their married lives, their attention turned to their relationship,' said Penny Mansfield, one of the sociologists.

'Prevailing opinions seem to stress independence and self-fulfilment and the importance of individual relationships.

'At the moment people have the worst of both worlds. In a way, it is not surprising they are bewildered.'

The nine-year project has taken place against a steadily-rising divorce rate.

There were 154,000 divorces in 1985, six times the number in 1960.

Projections from the latest figures estimate that one marriage in three today will end in divorce.

From the *Daily Telegraph*, 27 April 1988

ASSIGNMENTS ▷ ▷ ▷ ▷ ▷ ▷ ▷ ▷

1 In groups of four or five, discuss what you think the following phrases mean:
- 'it gives a purpose to lives and work'
- 'the burden of "freedom" that went with a single life'
- 'the romantic ideal of a perfect relationship'
- ' "the shackles" of domestic life'
- 'the abiding strength of marriage as an institution'.

2 What reasons can you give in your groups for:
- getting married,
- not getting married.

Make lists to compare with other groups.

3 How can you balance 'prevailing opinions' (independence, self-fulfilment) with marriage?

4 What have you learned from successful and unsuccessful marriages around you that can help equip you in the future?

BEING GAY

Coming to terms with our sexuality is one
of the keys to growing up. Accepting other
people's sexual orientation is equally
important. This extract is from the script of a
play that was considered too controversial
for the BBC to transmit during its usual
school programme times.

Scene 105: Classroom

*The class is laughing. Phil sits at the back of the class. A fifth
year group take more than the usual cursory interest in the
General Studies lesson. Mr Cross, the teacher, sits on the edge
of his desk. He's in his early thirties and fosters the image of
the still keen 'one of the lads'. The class is laughing because
someone has just uttered a slang word for 'homosexual' –
accepting Mr Cross's challenge to say them openly.*

FIRST GIRL   Homos.
FIRST BOY   Queers.
SECOND BOY   Poofs. Poofters. Perverts. Take your pick.
FIRST GIRL   Queen.
CROSS   Lesbians. Dykes. Girls do it as well, you know.

*The class giggle. Mr Cross slides off the desk and goes to the
blackboard.*

CROSS   (*writing the words as he speaks them*) Gays. Perverts. Deviants.
(*He turns back to the class.*) Hitler killed them. The Church
condemned them. Civilised society persecutes them.
FIRST BOY   You can get nicked for it, an' all.
CROSS   You can indeed, Dennis. Homosexuality can cost you your job,
your friends, your family. It can even cost you your freedom.

He returns to the blackboard and writes.
ONE IN TEN

CROSS   Recent surveys suggest that one teenager in ten is gay.
FIRST GIRL   Eh?
FIRST BOY   (*getting to his feet*) Alright, you lot . . . (*he scans the class*)
There's twenty of us in here. Play the white man, guys. Own
up. Both of you. Who is it, then?

The class laugh. Phil smiles.

SECOND BOY   We had one once. But he left.
FIRST GIRL   Matthew. He was . . . you know.
FIRST BOY   What she means is, he didn't fancy her.

BEING GAY

SECOND GIRL   (*to the boy*) Prat.

Cross takes a book ('One Teenager in Ten') from his desk.

CROSS   (*silencing the hub-bub*) I'm going to read something that might be of interest. Try to concentrate. (*He reads*) 'When I realised I was homosexual, the first thing I did was to sit down and cry . . .

CLASS   Ahhh . . .

CROSS   '. . . I wept for myself, but mostly I cried because I didn't conform. I couldn't be this way because it "just wasn't right". I wondered why the same sex attracted me . . .'

FIRST BOY   'Cos he was a pervert, that's why.

SECOND GIRL   (*sudden and surprising anger*) Shut up, Dennis!

The boy is nonplussed. Mr Cross considers the girl – smiles.

CROSS   Thank you, Vi.

SECOND GIRL   Well I think it's sad.

From Leslie Stewart, *The Two of Us*, BBC Filmscript, 1987

ASSIGNMENTS ▷ ▷ ▷ ▷ ▷ ▷ ▷ ▷

1 'I wondered why the same sex attracted me . . .' We are all at times attracted to people of the same sex. Why is this so?

2 How would you answer the question, 'How do you know if you are gay'?

3 Is it 'sad'?

4 Why does society use abusive language about gays? What do you think are other problems faced by gay people? What are the solutions?

PERSONAL SPACE

Do you prefer to be in a crowd or out on your own or does it depend on how you feel? Human beings are gregarious animals and generally need the society of others, and yet they need a feeling of personal space as well. Put people together in a group — in a school, or a block of flats, or on a beach — and they tend to assert these patterns. We learn from a young age to respect other people's privacy and to expect others to respect ours, even where the ways of gaining privacy may be very limited. We all need personal space to live in to some extent or other.

Personal space on the beach

ASSIGNMENTS ▷ ▷ ▷ ▷ ▷ ▷ ▷ ▷

1 Count the number of groups that you can see on this beach. In what ways do these people try to identify their own areas?

2 Would you prefer to be on a beach all on your own or with a lot of other people? How would you feel if one family came and sat right next to you or a few yards away? Try to explain your feelings.

3 Why do you think most of the people on this beach are in groups? How many are in each, or is there no typical size? What are the advantages and disadvantages to you of living in your family group, and do you feel that you have any 'private space' at home?

In the Shadow of Man

Many people are horrified when they hear that a chimpanzee might eat a human baby, but after all, so far as the chimpanzee is concerned, men are only another kind of primate, not so very different from baboons in *their* eyes. Surely it should be equally horrifying to reflect on the fact that in a great many places throughout their range chimpanzees are considered a delicacy by humans?

I myself have only seen the actual killing of a prey animal on two occasions: once on that far-off day when Hugo and I watched a red colobus monkey seized and torn to pieces, and once, four years later, when a juvenile baboon was caught on the outskirts of camp. That was much more spectacular.

It happened one morning when Rodolf, Mr McGregor, Humphrey* and an adolescent male were sitting, replete with bananas, and the baboon troop was passing through the camp area. All at once Rodolf got up and moved rapidly behind one of the buildings, followed by the other three. They all walked with the same silent, purposeful, almost stealthy pace that Figan had shown as he approached the palm tree that harboured his intended prey.

I followed – but even so I was too late to observe the actual capture. As I rounded the building I heard the sudden screaming of a baboon and then, a few seconds afterwards, the roaring of male baboons and the screaming and barking of chimpanzees. I ran the last few yards and, through some thick bushes, glimpsed Rodolf standing upright as he swung the body of a juvenile baboon above him by one of its legs and slammed its head down on to some rocks. Whether or not that was the actual death blow I could not tell: certainly the victim was dead as Rodolf, carrying it in one hand, set off rapidly up the slope.

The other chimps followed him closely, still screaming, and a number of adult male baboons continued to harass Rodolf, lunging towards him and roaring. This lasted only for a few minutes and then, to my surprise, they gave up. Presently the four chimpanzees appeared, climbing into the higher branches of a tall tree where Rodolf settled down and began to feed, tearing into the tender flesh of the belly and groin of his prey.

From Jane van Lawick-Goodall, *In the Shadow of Man*, Collins, 1971

*Rodolf, Mr McGregor, Humphrey and Figan are all chimpanzees studied by Jane van Lawick-Goodall.

ASSIGNMENTS ▷ ▷ ▷ ▷ ▷ ▷ ▷ ▷

1 Do you think that man is 'naturally' aggressive? What are your views about hunting for sport, and vegetarianism?

2 Why do you think that chimpanzees might attack other primates in particular? What do you think we can learn about the behaviour of man from the study of animals?

PERSONAL SPACE

The need for a parlour

The four-roomed houses usually provided both a living room and a more formal parlour, and fitted an even smaller scullery, a water-closet and perhaps a bath into a small rear projection.

This division of so small an overall floor area into so many rooms was not entirely of the architects' choosing. In 1902 Unwin had tried to reform the plan of the speculators' two-up, two-down house with its added tunnel-back, and he published his proposals in *Cottage Plans and Common Sense*. He tucked the scullery, water-closet and store cupboards of the rear extension into the main part of his proposed houses. At the same time he knocked together the parlour and living room into one larger and, he believed, more useful, lighter room . . . .'However desirable a parlour may be, it cannot be said to be necessary to health or family life,' he wrote; 'it is worse than folly to take space from that living-room, where it will be used every day and every hour, to form a parlour, where it will be used only once or twice a week.'

Unwin was possibly right about the needs of health but quite wrong about the needs of family life . . . .

The reformers in all their idealistic, socialist zeal wanted to improve people's health and to strengthen family life through the architectural agencies of beauty, sweetness and light. What they failed to realise was that families wanted to have a parlour or 'best room' both to accommodate their most treasured possessions and for formal occasions. It was closer to people's hearts. This need was a warning that rationalist, progressive architects should have heeded: a house can never be simply a machine for living in. It has to be a home.

From Antony Quiney, 'Come into my parlour', in *House and Home, A History of the Small English House*, BBC Publications, 1984

ASSIGNMENTS ▷ ▷ ▷ ▷ ▷ ▷ ▷ ▷

1 People in the 1900s preferred to have a smaller, second 'best' room rather than a larger living space in their houses. How do you use the space in your own home – which room is used for what? Do you like open-plan living areas? If you could add one more room what would it be used for?

2 Imagine a block of flats with one on each floor and ten floors. How do you think people would enjoy living there? Suggest ways to redesign the use of space to give a stronger sense of community.

3 With a partner, explain your requirements for your own ideal home, with drawings to meet your requirements. Compare plans in the group.

IMPROVE YOUR LEARNING

Do you enjoy learning? Are you making the most of skills you have already learned about learning? Have you realised you can learn how to learn?

A learning experience

'I remember trying to learn to ride, but the instructor was so two-faced. He was charming with my parents, but out in the field, once they had left, he was awful to us kids, really cruel. My parents just wouldn't believe us and thought we were just trying to get out of the lessons. In fact I didn't want to ride ever again.'

ASSIGNMENTS ▷ ▷ ▷ ▷ ▷ ▷ ▷ ▷

1 Jot down examples from your life of a good experience of learning and a bad experience. Also note down why they were so different.

2 With the person beside you, swop examples and see if you can work out what similarities there are in your experiences.

3 Join up with another pair so you are now in a group of four. Take two big pieces of paper and head one 'Constraints to learning' and the other 'Aids to learning'. Use your experiences to write down as many points as you can under these titles.

4 Pin these papers on the walls in your room and use them to discuss, as a large group:
   (a) points of relevance to your sixth form study;
   (b) what areas of your learning you can control, that is the areas you can do something about;
   (c) how you could change a poor learning pattern;
   (d) ways of removing constraints (for example, is there something you can do as a group?).

5 Tell a friend of one resolution you can adopt as a result of this activity.

TIME ALLOCATION

A timetable for a week

	12am	1am	2am	3am	4am	5am	6am	7am	8am	9am	10am	11am	12pm	1pm	2pm	3pm	4pm	5pm	6pm	7pm	8pm	9pm	10pm	11pm
Sun																								
Mon																								
Tue																								
Wed																								
Thu																								
Fri																								
Sat																								

A pie chart for twenty-four hours

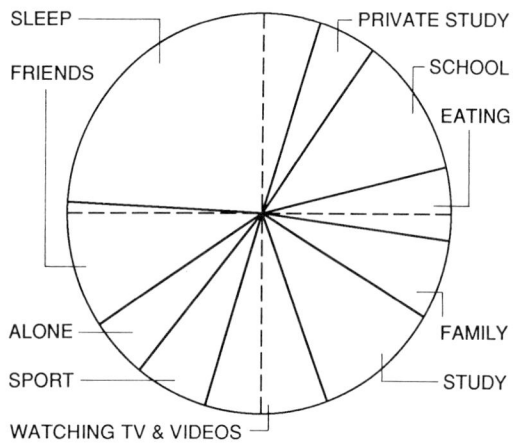

day into four quarters of six hours each. Calculate how many hours you spend on average per day:

- sleeping
- in school classes
- studying/doing research/homework
- relaxing with friend(s)
- relaxing with family including meals but not . . .
- watching TV/videos
- on sport/other exercise
- earning money
- alone, in ways not mentioned, for example, reading, bathing
- other activities.

ASSIGNMENTS ▷ ▷ ▷ ▷ ▷ ▷ ▷ ▷

1 Prepare a week's timetable like the one above and be as specific and as honest as possible about what you are usually doing at each hour of each day. Then transfer the information to a pie chart. The example above has divided a typical

2 Are you satisfied with the proportion of time you are spending on different areas of your life? How important is relaxation (sport, being alone, being with family, or with friends) to you? How important is study time?

3 Can you change the size of some of your slices? Draw your ideal pie chart.

Good study techniques?

- Avoid early morning?
- Study for half-an-hour at a time?
- Drink tea or coffee as you study so you don't require a break?
- Always study in the same place?
- Plan a week's study timetable in advance?
- Make sure the room is warm?
- Allocate time lengths for each task?
- Study for up to three hours at a time?
- Do not study past 10pm?
- Study with a friend?
- Offer yourself rewards as you finish a project?
- Start at least a week before a deadline?

ASSIGNMENTS ▷ ▷ ▷ ▷ ▷ ▷ ▷ ▷

1 In the sixth form you are expected to do some independent study. Look at the proposals in the box and discuss which of them represent good study techniques.

2 Draw up a new weekly timetable, based on the chart on page 46. Make sure you enter your study and relaxation commitments honestly. At the start of each term in the sixth form you could check this timetable, and make a new one if necessary.

DEADLINES

Keeping deadlines is part of everyday life. You could start this unit by naming the various deadlines you have had to keep this week. However, as for much of life, for work to be 'in on time', you need to plan ahead.

Meeting a deadline

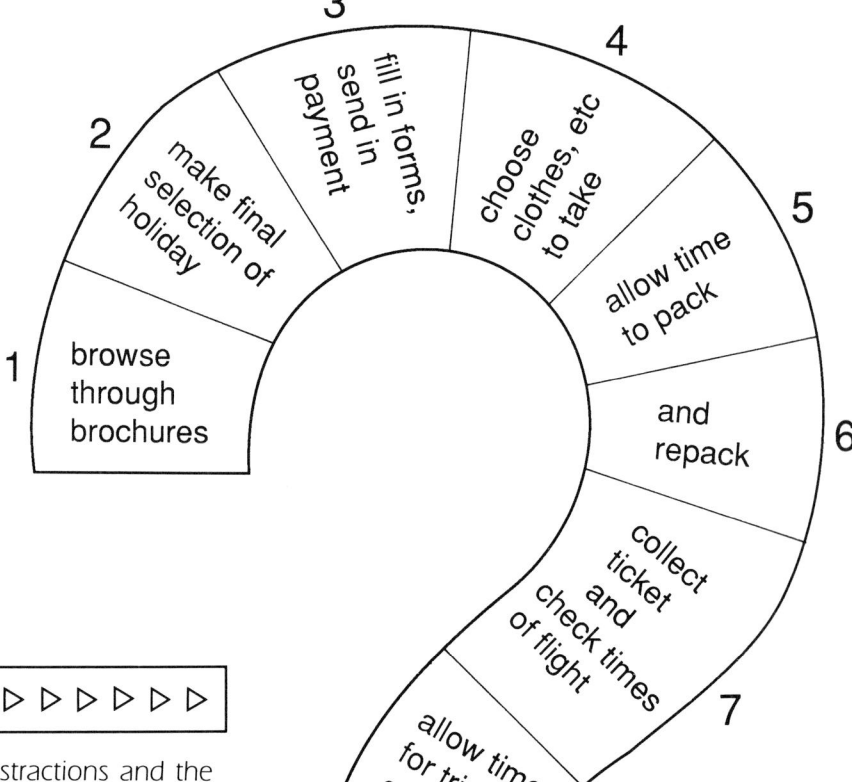

1 browse through brochures

2 make final selection of holiday

3 fill in forms, send in payment

4 choose clothes, etc to take

5 allow time to pack

6 and repack

7 collect ticket and check times of flight

8 allow time for trip to airport/station

9 flight/journey

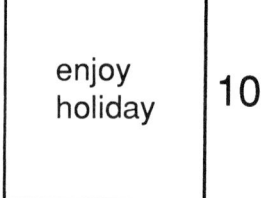

10 enjoy holiday

ASSIGNMENTS ▷ ▷ ▷ ▷ ▷ ▷ ▷ ▷

1 In pairs, what are the distractions and the serious problems that might get in the way of a person planning a holiday?

2 Be honest – name five things that stop you from getting down to work. Are these particular distractions when you are working at home or at school? How many of these are shown by the person planning a holiday? What implications can you draw from this?

3 Is it better to start a piece of work early and cover it gradually, divide it into manageable parts, or tackle it all in one go? How do you estimate the time you will need?

IMPROVE YOUR RESEARCH

Learning is not storing information. There is now so much information in every area of study that there is no point in trying to memorise it all, especially as it may be out of date tomorrow. But if you want to find out a piece of information, or learn more about something that interests you, you will have to know where to find a source of that particular knowledge. Your research may go along a variety of routes.

Knowing where to look

Which would you choose if you wanted to:

learn how to put up a bookshelf?
Would you:

☐ join a woodwork class?
☐ look for a carpenter in the yellow pages?
☐ borrow a book on woodwork?

find out the time a film starts?
Would you:

☐ phone the cinema?
☐ look in the newspaper?
☐ ask a friend?

find out names of hotels in Caernarvon?
Would you:

☐ phone Caernarvon information centre?
☐ find books in a library?
☐ write for the Welsh Tourist Board brochure?

check which video to buy?
Would you:

☐ visit different shops?
☐ read *Which?* guide?
☐ ask friends' opinions?

'I remember once reading that when someone asked Einstein what his phone number was, he went to the phone book to look it up.'

The young man laughed. 'You're kidding.'

'No, I'm not kidding. He said he never cluttered his mind with information he could find somewhere else.

'Now, if you didn't know better,' the manager continued, 'what would you think of someone who went to the phone book to look up his own number? Would you think he was a winner or a loser?'

The young man grinned and said, 'A real loser.'

'Of course you would,' the manager said. 'I would, too, but we'd be wrong, wouldn't we?'

The young man nodded his agreement.

From Kenneth Blanchard and Spencer Johnson, *One Minute Manager*, Fontana/Collins, 1983

ASSIGNMENTS ▷ ▷ ▷ ▷ ▷ ▷ ▷ ▷

1 Find out the differences between the following keys to any library:

- the author catalogue
- the title catalogue
- the subject catalogue
- the subject index
- the periodical catalogue

In pairs, design a flow chart with actual examples to show how to find the best books on a topic of your choice.

2 Write on a slip of paper something you would like to find out. For example: what are the dates of Easter and Diwali next year? How do I change my doctor?

Gather these questions in a hat and take turns to offer possible routes to learning the necessary information.

3 Discuss how to ask **effectively** on the phone and in person for information.

IMPROVE YOUR READING

Skimming a book

You may have used the word 'skim' to describe a bird's action of flying close to the surface of water, perhaps dipping to catch a fish. More commonly, you probably know the blue-topped milk bottles containing milk **skimmed** of cream. These two examples give you clues to the use of the term in reading; skimming is used to establish how useful a book will be to you: you can 'get the drift of it'.

ASSIGNMENTS ▷ ▷ ▷ ▷ ▷ ▷ ▷ ▷

1 Take a school textbook you are using and skim through it to see if it is sexist in its approach. Compare notes with a friend.

2 In pairs, discuss what else you learned as you skimmed through the book?

3 Somewhere in this book there is a poem by Adrian Mitchell. See if you can find it. Is it generally quicker to use a contents list or index than to skim? What does this tell you about reading a book for study purposes?

4 Ask your tutor to give you a book that is unfamiliar to you. First, note down what the title page, introduction and contents tell you about the subject of the book.

5 Write down a few specific questions you want answered through reading the above book. Be confident. You will usually find you know something about the topic. So you can set yourself specific goals. Now skim the book to find out what you need to know.

6 How do the last two exercises help you select a book from a library or a journal?

Scanning a page

If you want to find a phone number, you go as quickly as possible to the relevant page of a directory and look for particular details. Scanning is all about finding some specific information quickly. The assignments below illustrate how you already know how to vary your types of reading to suit your purpose. Just as a brain-scanner machine searches out matter needing attention, you **scan** a page for the particular information you require, give **more attention to some details**, but only note down **what you need**.

ASSIGNMENTS ▷ ▷ ▷ ▷ ▷ ▷ ▷ ▷

1 Scan the list opposite very quickly to see if there is a name with initials similar or close to your own.

2 Read the address out but only write down the phone number.

3 Do this exercise in pairs with a watch. One of you choose an **address** for the other to find and time the procedure.

4 Now use a visual guide, like a pencil, to help you, and time the procedure again. The guide should be moved smoothly along, but pointed just below the words you are reading. Discuss the effect it has on your reading efficiency.

5 Repeat Stage 3, but now watch your partner's eye movement closely. Which gives a more effective reading performance: lots of eye movement or keeping the eyes still?

6 Scan the passage on Einstein on page 49 and find what you think is the most relevant sentence.

IMPROVE YOUR READING

Students attending a car maintenance class

No.	SURNAME	INITIALS	MR. MRS. ETC.	ADDRESS	Tel. No.
				Subject *Car Maintenance*	
	NAME AND ADDRESS OF STUDENT				
1	Ashton	M.T.	Mrs	2 Giffin Way, Southford	579 1068
2	Bharadwa	M.A.	Ms	19 Dene Road, Greenholt	578 9306
3	Blaize	H.E.	Mr	22 Cavendish Gardens, Northwell	577 2111
4	Brar	Z.S.	Mr	12 Wood Road, Southford	579 9921
5	Catch	A.B.	Mrs	30 Craven Walk, Northwell	577 7029
6	Chahal	T.M.	Mr	10 Oldbridge Road, Oldbridge	571 0892
7	Chandjerath	A.M.	Mr	109 Lynton Ave, Northwell	577 2384
8	Da Silva	G.B.	Dr	2 Peterhead Court, Oldbridge	571 2660
9	Dhokia	P.M.	Miss	275a Woodhouse Ave, Greenholt	578 7847
10	Endersby	C.T.R.	Mr	Flat 5, 2a Common Rd, Greenholt	578 5324
11	Farrar	J.	Miss	11 Academy Gardens, Oldbridge	—
12	Hadler	J.P.	Miss	41 Raeburn Court, Southford	579 3296
13	Hurrel	E.	Mrs	43 Raeburn Court, Southford	579 9879
14	James	L.	Miss	90 Darwin Rd, Northwell	577 9971
15	Kavanagh	P.P.	Mr	10 Radcliffe Way, Greenholt	578 5757
16	Khan	J.S.	Mr	2 Hazeltree Lane, Southford	579 1967
17	Killeen	T.C.	Mrs	7 Marine Court, Marine Cres, Oldbridge	—
18	Koong	Q.	Ms	154 North Road, Northwell	577 1272
19	Mayar	B.R.	Miss	70 Grange Court, Old Southford Rd, Southford	579 6937
20	Murphy	W.L.	Mr	7 Magnolia Court, 60 Moriston Way, Northwell	577 2084
21	Narwan	G.	Mr	9 West Close, Oldbridge	—
22	Page	D.	Mrs	57 Church Lane, Greenholt	578 5105
23	Pollock	B.G.P.	Mr	30 Townsend Ave, Northwell	577 5641
24	Rinaldi	D.	Ms	3 Melrose Ave, Oldbridge	571 1944
25	Szijarto	H.N.	Miss	50 Milton Ave, Oldbridge	571 9651
26	Thompson	A.M.	Miss	44 Swallow Drive, Oldbridge	571 5372
27	Wegrzynski	P.L.	Miss	9a Newbury Cres, Northwell	577 3498
28	Woltenholte	F.	Mr	112 Dorchester Road, Southford	579 4078

IMPROVE YOUR READING

Faster reading

Do you think you read more slowly than other people? Faster reading is a skill you can work on. Try this set of exercises with a partner.

ASSIGNMENTS ▷ ▷ ▷ ▷ ▷ ▷ ▷ ▷

1 One of you hold the book in front of you just above eye level, and look at the page opposite to concentrate on the introduction to a local guide book.

2 First, read a few lines very slowly, so that you stop on every syllable of every word.

3 Then, read the next lines very, very fast. While you are doing this, your partner will watch how your eyes move, and when you have finished describe the different performances.

4 Reverse roles. Then repeat the fast read, taking in three or more words at each 'visual stop' or eye fixation.

5 Read on in the passage at your normal studying speed and ask your partner to note any of the following habits:
   • mouthing the words
   • back-tracking
   • wandering eyes
   • many eye fixations.
   Are these good habits? Say why or why not.

6 Finally, each of you practise deliberately fixing your eyes on specific points of the passage and see all the words from these points. Three to four eye fixations should be sufficient to read a long line of print. One may be enough for a column. The more you do this the faster and more efficiently you will read.

IMPROVE YOUR READING

Ealing walkabout

IN THE DAYS before maps and guide books, stories about people and events in the eight Middlesex villages that now constitute the London Borough of Ealing, were retold over the centuries during the parochial **Perambulation** – an ancient ceremony dating back to Roman times, and reinforced by Elizabeth I. She ordered that once a year, usually in Ascension Week, the residents of every parish were to gather at the parish church (then the centre of village life), and follow the vicar and other local dignitaries in procession around the parish boundaries. Willow wands were distributed for beating the boundary line the whole length of its course (even in the middle of the River Brent), and the exact position of boundary posts and stones was forcibly impressed on succeeding generations of parishioners by bumping their heads against them. Except for these minor inconveniences, the Perambulation offered a jolly day's outing: stops were made at inns and places of interest along the way, there was gossip, lusty singing of hymns, and a free meal provided by the parish authorities. The practice of 'beating the bounds' was thus a relatively painless way of ensuring that land was not sneakily encroached on by neighbouring parishes, and that local legends were kept alive as times and places changed.

Such a simple custom could not survive the massive changes brought about by the 20th century, however. The annual 'walkabout' gradually died out as villages grew into towns; the responsibility for parish administration was transferred from the church to local boards, and wider authorities; and old boundary marks were buried under the spread of suburbia. Thanks to modern administration and communications, residents in today's towns undoubtedly enjoy a higher standard of living than their counterparts of a century ago – the majority of whom suffered bad sanitation, poor education and severe poverty. But, as small rural parishes merged into urban districts, and the districts were in turn absorbed into boroughs, individuality was swept away with the old boundary lines, and community spirit (with a few rare exceptions) was destroyed by the ever-increasing numbers of new residents from other towns, counties and even countries.

On April Fools' Day 1965, the Municipal Boroughs of **Southall, Acton** and **Ealing** (which already included **Hanwell, Greenford, Northolt, Perivale** and **West Twyford**) were amalgamated to form the new **London Borough of Ealing** – one of 32 such administrative units to be created in Greater London by the London Government Act of 1963. Over 300,000 people fell under the jurisdiction of the new borough, making Ealing – in terms of population size – the fifth largest London Borough and one of the biggest urban administrative areas in the whole of England and Wales. Perambulations and *Progress* simply do not go together, and there's no point in bewailing the fact. But the personality of a place depends on the extent to which its legacy from the past has been incorporated into new developments, and by forsaking the old principle of '*looking backwards*' in favour of *Unity* and standardisation, we are in danger of losing something much more important than a few out-of-date

IMPROVE YOUR READING

boundary lines and the quaint custom that maintained them. If the remaining traces of the borough's heritage are to be preserved, we must first appreciate them; and there is therefore an urgent need for today's residents to understand something of the way in which people and events of the past have influenced the emergence of the towns they live in, and the character of their borough as a whole.

From Kate McEwan, *Ealing Walkabout*, Nick Weatley Associates, 1983

ASSIGNMENTS ▷ ▷ ▷ ▷ ▷ ▷ ▷ ▷

You may not have actually read for understanding as you tried the exercises on page 52. Now put all these points together to help you learn more successfully from your reading. Answer these questions in pairs using this extract.

(a) **Library usage**

If you wanted to borrow the book *Ealing Walkabout* by Kate McEwan from a library, what steps would you take?

(b) **Skimming**

What would you expect to learn if you bought it?

(c) **Scanning and faster reading**

Why did 'Perambulation' not survive?

(d) **Research**

Finally, divide into small groups to find out about some ancient ceremony in your own neighbourhood. Each group should take – and keep to – one particular research technique (for example, one might talk to older residents, another, phone a local conservation society). You could make a list of the techniques first, and afterwards discuss which way was the most fruitful. Your research might of course make an interesting piece to give to a school assembly.

IMPROVE YOUR LISTENING

Before we learn to talk as children, most of us have heard the world around us. A baby can usually hear from the moment of birth, and many scientists and mothers suspect babies sense sound vibrations while they are still in the womb. But while most babies clearly hear sounds, the ones they **listen** to are the sounds of people talking. It is a sad fact that most of us, as we grow older, do not listen as closely as we should to people talking. Listening is, after all, a vital skill in learning and in life, and we need to think about how to listen without being distracted even when we think the subject matter is boring!

This unit is designed to make you more aware of how you listen and react, in a dialogue, in a group, and in order to learn.

The cartoon below was drawn by Bateman and published in *The Tatler* in 1920.

IMPROVE YOUR LISTENING

Non-verbal communication

'Smile!' That's what you are always told when you are in front of a camera. And it is not difficult to work out why. But it is not only with your mouth's expression that you communicate to others. The activities which follow give you a chance to consider the effect of body language generally, but first of all look at the chart below and consider how people give the four signals listed on the left.

You signal:	By the following non-verbal communication:					
	posture	tone	mouth	distance	eyes	hands
WARMTH						
HOSTILITY						
DOMINATION						
SUBMISSIVENESS						

ASSIGNMENTS ▷ ▷ ▷ ▷ ▷ ▷ ▷ ▷

1 Copy the chart into your exercise book and write a brief description in each box. For example for showing warmth with your mouth you could write 'smiling'.

2 **The Focus Game**
   To give yourself something to talk about, write down points to finish these two sentences:

'I feel best when I am with people who . . . .'
'I feel worst when I am with people who . . . .'
Divide into groups of four. Each of you is to be given the full attention and close focus of two members of the group for five minutes, while he or she talks only about, and answers questions only about, the above sentences.

IMPROVE YOUR LISTENING

It is important that you do not shift the focus to yourself or express disagreement if you are not the focus person. The point is to encourage the focus person and to understand her or his feelings.

The fourth person should draw up a checklist like the one below on a sheet of paper and apply it to one of the listeners. Make sure there is a sheet for each person in the group.

When all have had a turn, decide which of you was the best **listener** in your group, and discuss with other groups why this should be so. Is that person also a 'good communicator'? Can you answer the question: what makes 'a good listener'?

Checklist for behaviour observed

1 Suggestion seeking								
2 Suggestion giving								
3 Supporting								
4 Telling								
5 Clarification seeking								
6 Clarification giving								
7 Summarising								
8 Agreeing specific action								
9 Pointing out difficulties								
10 Disagreeing								
11 Criticising								
12 Time allocation								

3 Non-verbal communications

After you have filled in the chart on non-verbal communications on page 57, you can find out what image you project by asking someone to watch you from behind a window! Half your group hold a discussion on a controversial topic like 'the most serious problem in your school or college'. The other half watch from a place out of earshot but within sight. Each of you focus on a friend and write notes on how he or she is communicating non-verbally, while listening and while speaking. Be prepared to accept criticisms in your turn.

Or your tutor could arrange for someone to tape or video a discussion you have as a group and see what you learn from it afterwards.

4 In small groups, perform these two tasks:
   (a) Think of captions for the 1920 Bateman cartoon.
   (b) Write a list of ways that help you listen in a learning situation. You could start by assessing the classes in which you enjoy/do not enjoy listening.

5 Group dynamics

This activity can be tried after questions 1–4 above, or taken at random after any small group discussion.

Answer honestly about your group:
   (a) Who talked the most?
   (b) Who talked the least?
   (c) Was there a leader?
   (d) Were these people also good listeners?
   (e) Have you become 'set' in a role within group work (for example, the note taker; the joker)? How can you change this?
   (f) How efficiently did you work as a group?
   (g) How could you have improved your working together?

IMPROVE YOUR TALKING

Greetings and questions

Isn't it odd that many people find spoken language more difficult than written? We learn to talk before we learn to write, and for most of the day we chat easily to our family or friends. But put us in a room of strangers, or a formal situation, and we become tongue-tied. This need not be the case, for there is an art to be learned in making confident speeches, or easy conversation with people who may, after all, become friends. There is a skill too in asking questions to help you learn.

Certainly, far greater emphasis is given today to spoken language and it is important to be able to communicate verbally in a way that is appropriate to the situation.

ASSIGNMENTS ▷ ▷ ▷ ▷ ▷ ▷ ▷ ▷

1 Your tutor will need to set up this activity for you as you require some sort of intercom system between adjoining rooms. Half the group goes in one room, while the other half goes in a room next door. Take it in turns to talk to someone in the other room. You must find out to whom you are talking by asking questions that do not include, 'What's your name?' When you have discovered the identity, say goodbye and jot the name down on a piece of paper. While you are doing this the person behind you in the queue takes notes on your performance. These should cover:

   (a) the introduction, for example, how does the person establish contact/trust?
   (b) style, for example, how interested/polite is the speaker?
   (c) relevance of questioning, for example, how long does it take to establish identity?

   Afterwards, the person who has made the notes should pass them to the person concerned and discuss as a group what made for successful interaction and information-gathering.

2 On a slip of paper write down your name and an activity, hobby or sport you are particularly good at, or enjoy regularly. Put all the slips in a hat or box and take it in turns to pull out a slip. Then ask questions of the 'expert' to find out as much as possible about how you too could take up this pastime. The group meanwhile assesses your performance.

   Discuss afterwards what you learned about asking questions.

IMPROVE YOUR TALKING

Negotiations

ASSIGNMENTS ▷ ▷ ▷ ▷ ▷ ▷ ▷ ▷

1 What common ground brings the parties shown in each of these photographs into negotiation with each other? What skills do you need in order to be successful at negotiating with other people?

2 Choose two or four members of your group to act out each of the situations represented in the photographs, and to continue their negotiations for a few minutes. The rest of the group should

watch, and then comment on the argument, patience, powers of persuasion, and, in the terms used by American diplomats, 'leverage' on each other.

3 Suppose that you are unable to complete a major piece of work in time to meet a teacher's deadline. How would you go about 'negotiating' for a time extension?

IMPROVE YOUR TALKING

Formal speeches

The speeches below are taken from a television play that is set at a school's farewell disco party for a retiring member of staff, James. As you will see from his speech James did not accept early retirement voluntarily. Andrew is a pupil, who has the job of thanking James.

ANDREW   So finally, to all those teachers who have done so much for us and have helped us get off to a good start in the world, I would like to say thank you very much on behalf of all the pupils . . .

JAMES   Headmaster, colleagues. I did have a speech, carefully prepared, but somehow tonight there are other things I'd rather say instead. You must all envy me, retiring, and you'll think me a fool if I say I don't want to go. But it's not quite the same when things are forced upon you. I thought I was valued, and still doing a useful job. The Headmaster thought otherwise.

The head referred to me in his speech as a man of the past – may I say with equal warmth that he is a man of the future. The bright hard future of the Eighties – rather like your disco, Headmaster: all very well if you're out in the middle enjoying yourself, but not much fun if you're watching from the side.

I'm not to do the decent thing, getting out of the way gracefully – I'm just here to say goodbye . . .

So goodbye, Headmaster, from all of us you've sent out into the world, with nowhere much to go, and no one much to care.

From Chris Ellis, 'Just Deserts' in *Scene Scripts 5*, Longman

ASSIGNMENTS ▷ ▷ ▷ ▷ ▷ ▷ ▷ ▷

1 First, in pairs, write the earlier part of Andrew's speech. One of you could then give the speech to the class who can discuss its content, style and delivery.

2 What do you think of James's speech? Rewrite it for a teacher who is ready and willing to take retirement.

3 Would this dialogue have been different if delivered by female characters?

4 As a class, list the occasions when, traditionally, people are involved in speech-making. Then, in pairs, prepare a speech to give to the class, but do not tell them beforehand for what occasion the speech has been prepared. Consider the following points:

- its appropriateness to the audience on that occasion;
- content – whether or not it matters what is said;
- the style – how sincere you are;
- the delivery – did you write it all out, or make notes, or ad-lib? Which is more successful?

COPING WITH CRITICISM

'Fogging'

In order to cope with criticism, it is important not to become defensive. It is all too easy to react negatively and passively to criticism. 'Fogging' is a technique developed by Eric Berne that allows you to acknowledge to your critic that there may be some truth in the criticism but allows you to remain the judge of what you do.

ASSIGNMENTS ▷ ▷ ▷ ▷ ▷ ▷ ▷ ▷

1 In groups of four, write on three pieces of paper the three words 'assertive', 'passive' and 'aggressive'. Then, for five minutes, hold 'a brain-storming session' allocating different terms to each type of behaviour. At the end of five minutes select one definition that sums up each for your group.

2 One of you then takes this definition to another group. With the 'envoy' discuss what you think of the definition for a few minutes.

3 Next the envoy returns to report to her or his original group.

4 As a large group discuss how you felt in stage 2 and 3. How did you, for instance, give/cope with criticism of the new definitions?

5 In pairs, role-play a scene in which one person is being critical, but the other is trying:
   - not to deny any criticism;
   - not to get defensive;
   - not to counter-attack.

   Now try out the scene so that the criticism is more constructive.

6 As a group discuss the techniques you have learned.

HOW TO TAKE NOTES

Taking notes from a speaker

Taking notes from books and journals is a skill you may be developing already. Good note-taking is certainly an art that improves with practice; the more you study the more likely you are to write notes both from written material and from lectures.

When you listen to someone on the phone, taking a message in note-form probably causes you no problems. You can stop and ask the speaker to repeat a point or to go more slowly, or you can add some verbal remark yourself so as to give yourself time to jot down the necessary points.

When you are listening to a formal lecture, it is more difficult to interrupt the speaker. The very length of the lecture and the density of the subject matter may make note-taking seem more difficult. In fact, a good speaker will often introduce a lecture by outlining the topics to be covered in the order you can expect them, in much the same way as the media give you the headlines first. This can help you organise your notes at once.

It is also worth remembering that most people repeat themselves when communicating. They (as here!) frequently say the same thing twice, varying the words they used in the first instance.

The aim of this unit is to introduce you to techniques that can help you record the information you need for future reference. Remember notes are for you alone, to help *you* understand and remember points. There is no one correct way of taking notes, but the better organised you are the better your learning will be.

Ten guides to good listening
1 Find an area of interest.
2 Judge content, not delivery.
3 Hold your fire.
4 Listen for ideas.
5 Be flexible.
6 Work at listening.
7 Resist distractions.
8 Exercise your mind.
9 Keep your mind open.
10 Capitalise on thought speed.

ASSIGNMENTS ▷ ▷ ▷ ▷ ▷ ▷ ▷ ▷

1 Consider the 'Ten guides to good listening'. What do you think each means? (For instance, the point about 10 is that while most people speak at about 125 words per minute, most people think at about four times that rate.)

2 Look at the list of word cues, and find others that indicate:
   • comparison and/or contrast
   • addition
   • cause and effect
   • opposition
   • chronological order.

3 Either record in advance or agree as a group on a particular news broadcast you will take notes on as you are listening. Compare your results to assess how you could improve your system.

4 Apply the same exercise to a particular lesson that a group of you attend together.

Word cues

Speakers often give you clues to help you or to signal what is coming next. Here are some examples:

Important bit ahead:

> 'An <u>important</u> point...'
> 'A <u>major</u> factor...'
> 'A <u>significant</u> development...'
> 'The <u>essential</u> cause...'

Lists come next:

> 'The three vital factors...'
> 'Remember the five causes...'

A new subject follows:

> 'This led to...'
> 'A clear development was...'
> 'Let us see what happened next...'
> 'This proves...'
> 'So...'

Conclusion:

> 'Finally...'
> 'In conclusion...'
> 'To sum up...'

5 What problems did you experience in trying to concentrate on the speaker? Suggest ways to help each other overcome the problems.

6 Share the many symbols and forms of abbreviation of words that you know. Think about useful abbreviations in different subjects.

HOW TO TAKE NOTES

Taking notes from written material

The following extract considers how children
can be socialised by their parents into
gender roles at a very young age. It is
followed by examples of three systems for
making notes on the passage.

Differential socialisation

There is an interesting study (Smith and Lloyd, 1978) on parent differential
treatment of boys and girls and the age of their own children depending on
whether they believe they are interacting with a boy or a girl. Six-month-old
children were dressed as a boy or a girl and given names appropriate to their
dress. If the adults thought they were playing with a boy, large body
movements on the part of the child were interpreted as a playful motion and
the adult responded with play. If a similar movement was made by a
supposed girl, the adults interpreted it as a frightened movement and gave
the child support and cuddled 'her'.

Again, this work has not been done on parents playing with their own
children; it would be impossible to do such a study.

There is one area where differential socialisation has been documented
which may have wide implications. We do know that boys and girls are given
different kinds of toys and, more importantly, fathers initiate sex-appropriate
play with children when sex-typed toys are available. Further, at some ages
but not others, if boys are playing with 'girl' toys they will be punished for it
(Langlois and Downs, 1980).

Mothers are more likely to play with 'girl' toys when they are with their sons
or their daughters and neither mothers nor fathers punish daughters when
they are doing cross-sex-toy play. Much of the differential socialisation studies
have concentrated on the mothers, reasoning that mothers spend more time
with the children. With further work on the fathers, more differential
socialisation may become evident.

From Carol Nagy Jacklin, 'Boys and Girls Entering School' in *Sex Differentiation and
Schooling*, M. Marland (ed.), Heinemann Educational Books, pp. 13–14

HOW TO TAKE NOTES

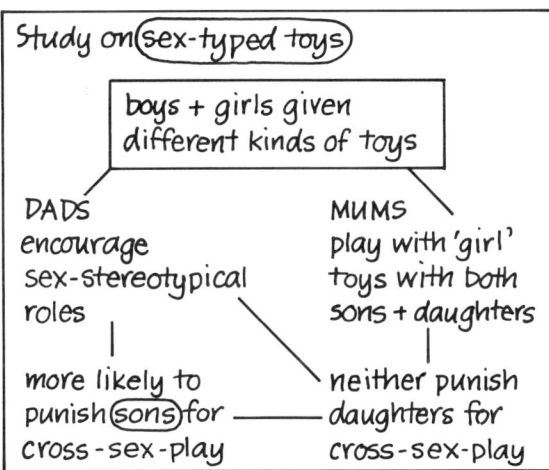

Study by Smith + Lloyd 1978
- 6 month child dressed as boy
or girl to play with adult

(a) if thought boy:
    large body movements
    thought "playful" → play

(b) if thought girl:
    same movements
    thought "fearful" → cuddle

N.B. Can't be done with parents'
own children.

Study on (sex-typed toys)

    boys + girls given
    different kinds of toys

DADS   MUMS
encourage   play with 'girl'
sex-stereotypical   toys with both
roles   sons + daughters

more likely to   neither punish
punish (sons) for ───── daughters for
cross-sex-play   cross-sex-play

treatment ... boy ... girl

toys ... dad ... boy ... girl

mum boy girl ... teddies + dolls ... dad (no)

ASSIGNMENTS ▷ ▷ ▷ ▷ ▷ ▷ ▷ ▷

1 Look at the systems that are used to
  make notes from the passage 'Differential
  socialisation'. Discuss the relative value of
  each. Can you think of others?

2 Try out a different system like a star, or
  splay chart, for each of the two topics in
  the passage.

3 Find the passage from 'Ealing Walkabout'
  on page 53 of this book and prepare
  your own notes on it.

4 Compare your notes with those made by
  others, first in pairs, then in fours, and
  consider the following questions:
  • Did you use one piece of paper or lots
    of cards?
  • How did you decide what was
    important?
  • Did you use a drawing, diagram or a
    linear structure?
  • What are the advantages and
    disadvantages of each?
  • Did you use a system, full sentences,
    key words?
  • What could you have cut out from your
    notes and what should you have
    added?
  • How could you have used arrows,
    colours, outlining or underlining to
    improve your notes?
  • Did you record the source of your notes
    for future reference?

5 Finally, in pairs, make notes on what you
  have learned from this exercise. Check
  yours with others in a full group.

IMPROVE YOUR WRITING

Essay writing becomes an increasingly important part of your work in the sixth form. Outside school you may find yourself writing letters that require almost as much planning and attention to detail.

Careful preparation

You will have realised that careful preparatory work is the key to successful writing. If you have decided to decorate your bedroom, you do not start the next moment with the first pot of paint you come across. You consult paint and wallpaper charts (and anyone you share the room with!) to choose your colour scheme; you collect a ladder, brushes and other essential equipment around you; you clean the room and wash or strip the walls, and so on. All of this preparatory work takes as much time – if not more time – as the actual decorating period. But it is hardly wasted time. So it is with organising your knowledge and thoughts before attempting to write an essay or letter.

Essay writing summary

Rather than summarise what I have said, I leave the task to eight Italian boys with little education but lots of sense:

'To start with, each of us keeps a notebook in his pocket. Every time an idea comes up, we make a note of it. Each idea on a separate sheet, on one side of the page.

Then one day we gather together all the sheets of paper and spread them on a big table. We look through them, one by one, to get rid of duplications. Next, we make separate piles of the sheets that are related, and these will make up the chapters. Every chapter is sub-divided into small piles, and they will become paragraphs.

At this point we try to give a title to each paragraph. If we can't it means either that the paragraph has no content or that too many things are squeezed into it. Some paragraphs disappear. Some are broken up. While we name the paragraphs we discuss their logical order, until an outline is born. With the outline set, we organise all the piles to follow its pattern.

We take the first pile, spread the sheets on the table, and we find the sequence for them. And so we begin to put down a first draft of the text. We duplicate that part so that we each can have a copy in front of us. Then, scissors, paste and coloured pencils. We shuffle it all again. New sheets are added. We duplicate again.

A race begins now for all of us to find any word that can be crossed out, any excess adjectives, repetitions, lies, difficult words, over-long sentences, and any two concepts that are forced into one sentence.

We call in one outsider after another. We prefer it if they have not had too much schooling. We ask them to read aloud. And we watch to see if they have understood what we meant to say.

IMPROVE YOUR WRITING

We accept their suggestions if they clarify the text. We reject any suggestions made in the name of caution.

Having done all this hard work and having followed these rules that anyone can use, we often come across an intellectual idiot who announces, "This letter has a remarkably personal style."

Why don't you admit that you don't know what the art of writing is? It is an art that is the very opposite of laziness.'

Quoted on the inside front cover of *Letter to a Teacher* by the School of Barbiana. English translation in Penguin Books 1970.

ASSIGNMENTS ▷ ▷ ▷ ▷ ▷ ▷ ▷ ▷

1 Use the 'Essay writing summary' prepared by the Italian boys to make notes on how to write an essay.

2 Discuss how these points can be made relevant to your own work. What, for instance, do you find the most difficult part of writing an essay? Is there anything you would wish to add?

3 Choose one of the essays from the General Studies paper on pages 72–3 and take fifteen minutes to prepare an outline.

4 Some popular American books on 'how to do' various activities present the material as questions and answers. What is the value of doing this?

5 Write down the title of a piece of work you have recently been given to do. Now write as many questions as you can that you think need answering in order to complete the work. Can you reorder them? How is this helpful for you starting a piece of work? Discuss your questions with a friend.

IMPROVE YOUR WRITING

Sequencing material

Having obtained the information for an essay or document, it is important to present the information in a logical sequence.

ASSIGNMENTS ▷ ▷ ▷ ▷ ▷ ▷ ▷ ▷

1 On your own put the paragraphs from 'The case for nursery education' below in the order you think best.

2 Discuss your decisions with a friend.

The case for nursery education

Despite these facts, the 1980 Education Act weakened the obligations of local education authorities to provide nursery education, so formally downgrading the status and importance of the service. This had already suffered nationally from the effects of the cutbacks in public sector spending of the late 1970s.

Nursery education should not be seen as simply providing childcare, nor be thought of as merely a preparation for infant school. Good nursery education is in itself of value providing experiences appropriate to the particular age and development of three- and four-year-olds.

The 1978 Warnock Report put forward under-fives provision for children with special educational needs as a priority recommendation and suggested that there should be a greater expansion of nursery education for all children. Nursery teachers are often the first to recognise under-fives who have learning difficulties.

Furthermore, the majority of parents seek pre-school education for their children in preference to other forms of pre-school provision (Bone 1977, Lewisham Pre-School Survey 1982, Greenwich Pre-School Survey 1987).

Studies show that children who attend nursery schools and classes do better in statutory school (Boehm 1970, Lazar and Darlington 1982, Sylva and Jowett 1986). Research also suggests that high quality early childhood education can lead to lasting improvements in education, employment and social responsibility within the community (Schweinhart and Weikhart 1980, Woodhead 1985).

Nursery education, despite its non-statutory and discretionary nature, should be seen in Tower Hamlets as an educational priority area. The following two pages outline some of the achievements in nursery education in Inner London over the past ten years. It is to be hoped that none of this service will be eroded by the disbandment of the ILEA.

'Young children are important in their **own right** and as our resource for the future. High quality provision in health care and education is a right of all children and a long-term investment in the country's future.' (Under-Fives Unit, National Children's Bureau.)

Many children living in the inner city, especially, suffer disadvantage through disruptions to family life such as poor housing, overcrowding, isolation, poverty, ill health and unemployment. These circumstances are particularly significant for children under five.

REVISION TECHNIQUES

Examinations are part of everyone's life at school. You may already have taken some exams, and, if you plan to go on to further study, you will inevitably face exams again. This unit gives you the chance to stop and think about how you might improve on your revision techniques for the future.

A significant factor in passing any exam is knowing exactly what is expected of you. It is a good idea to look at the syllabus, and to obtain past examination papers in your subject(s).

ASSIGNMENTS ▷ ▷ ▷ ▷ ▷ ▷ ▷ ▷

1 How long was your revision period before your last exams? Would you revise for a longer or shorter time before your next exams? How do higher level exams demand more from you?

2 Did you establish a timetable? Was this weekly or daily? How would you advise someone to keep to a routine? Who did you ask to help you to keep to yours, and in what ways?

3 What do you remember that most got in the way of settling down to revise? Can you find a solution to this now?

4 How would you improve your powers of concentration now? Are your revision habits going to be different from your study habits?

5 What did you find a particularly helpful revision technique before your last exams?

6 What sort of written revision worked best for you?

7 Did you 'spot' questions? Would you do it again?

8 How did you best prepare for:
   (a) essay questions?
   (b) practical questions?
   (c) oral questions?

9 Did your eating, exercise or sleeping habits change before the exams? What would you recommend to someone about to take exams?

10 How did you deal with exam nerves?

Look at the exam paper on pages 72–3 and then do the following assignments.

ASSIGNMENTS ▷ ▷ ▷ ▷ ▷ ▷ ▷ ▷

1 On your own think about and jot down some points on the exam questions overleaf in the light of your own experience, and then discuss your answers with the whole group. Draw up a list of strategies for your revision time.

2 Look at the specimen exam paper. Analyse it, so as to advise a candidate on:
   • the arrangement of questions;
   • the types of questions;
   • the time allocated to each section.

3 In groups of those of you taking the same course, or studying the same subject, look closely at the relevant past papers and consider the points above.

4 Take an essay title each and for fifteen minutes prepare (in writing) an **outline** of your possible answer. Read it out to the group to criticise and add information.

SUMMER 1982

223

GENERAL STUDIES

9375/1,2,3
8000/1,2,3

ADVANCED LEVEL

GENERAL PAPER

ORDINARY LEVEL (A0)

(Two hours and a half)

Write on one subject selected from each of the Papers 1, 2 and 3, i.e. on three subjects in all. For each subject, either write a composition or answer as required. Answers should be 400-500 words in length.

You are advised to divide your time equally among the three answers.

Begin each subject on a fresh sheet of paper, giving at the head your name, index-number and the number of the Paper (1, 2 or 3). If you are unable to answer a question in any one Paper, send in a blank sheet giving your name, index-number and the number of that Paper (1, 2 or 3).

N.B. *Supervisors are requested to place the answers belonging to the three Papers in separate envelopes, which should be marked 1, 2 or 3.*

PAPER 1

1.

2.

3.   What are the advantages and disadvantages of Sixth Form Colleges?

4.   To what extent should a country make special provision for ethnic minorities within its population?

224   EXAMINATION PAPERS (ADVANCED LEVEL)

5.

6. Do you feel yourself to be a European? Should you?

PAPER 2

7. To what extent are the traditional distinctions between the various scientific disciplines now out-moded?

8. What scope is there for re-cycling used materials?

9.

10. Discuss the various methods of heat insulation applied to our homes these days.

11. What would be the pros and cons of being able to determine the sex of an unborn child?

12. Explain the importance of the earth's atmosphere and the effects that possible changes might have.

PAPER 3

13. Account for the popularity of **one** of the following: *(a)* coin-collecting, *(b)* stamp-collecting, *(c)* flower-arranging, *(d)* bell-ringing.

14. What are the essential differences between the presentation of a play on the stage and one on film?

15. Which emotions is music especially fitted to express?

EXAM TECHNIQUES

However much you know when you enter an exam, you can fail it through simple 'mechanical' faults like not reading the instructions, not reading the whole paper through, and taking longer than you should to answer a question. Why are these factors so vital and what can you do about them?

On pages 75 and 76 there are two extracts from study guides and in the next column there is a list of common key words in examinations. Read through the material and then do the assignments.

Common key words in exams

account	evaluate
analyse	explain
assess	illustrate
brief	interpret
calculate	justify
comment	list
compare	outline
contrast	prove
consider	reconcile
criticise	relate
define	review
describe	state
detailed	summarise
discuss	trace
enumerate	view

ASSIGNMENTS ▷ ▷ ▷ ▷ ▷ ▷ ▷ ▷

1 One of the most common faults in exams is a failure to answer a question precisely. Look at the extract from 'Strengthening Your Study Skills' and then prepare the same, very detailed breakdown of a question you have been set in a class recently. Compare this with a friend's attempt.

2 Look at the list of common key words in exams and divide the words amongst you to find out the meaning and implications for an essay. Add any others that are used in questions set in exams.

3 Do you agree with the timing allowed in the table in the extract 'Allocation of time in an examination'? How do *you* divide up the time? Develop Table 3 to cover other time lengths.

4 There are three steps you might take before you start on a question in an exam, **within** the time you allocate to 'planning your answer'. What are they?

5 If you are taking practical and oral examinations, you should reconsider these questions in terms of your needs.

Strengthening your study skills

1. **Describe** and **discuss** the major **educational reforms** initiated during the last **30 years**.

In this examination question the most logical plan is first to list chronologically the educational reforms you will discuss (*introduction*) and then *describe* and *discuss* each in detail (*body paragraphs*). Finally, make some general remarks about the outcome (*results*) of these reforms in your *conclusion*. Your outline might look something like this:

I. The major educational reforms initiated during the last 30 years were:

    A.)
    B.)   Chronological list
    C.)

II. The first of these reforms involved a change in . . . . (*description*)

    A. The reason for the reform . . . .
    B. The person (group) responsible for the reform . . . .
    C. The reform was implemented . . . .
    D. It resulted in . . . .

III. The second reform involved . . . . (*description*)

    A. It was caused by . . . .
    B. Although it was opposed by . . . .
    C. It was implemented . . . .
    D. The end results . . . .

IV. The third of these reforms . . . .

    A. It was proposed by . . . . because . . . . . .
    B. It was implemented . . . .
    C. It caused . . . .

V. These reforms modernised the educational system and helped broaden the system in . . . . (country). It helped the schools prepare . . . .

From Suzanne Salimbene, *Strengthening Your Study Skills*, University of London, Institute of Education, 1982, pp. 92–3

Allocation of time in an examination

Table 1 Allocating your time in examination

Time allowed for examination	Number of questions to be answered	Available for each question	
		Time*	Marks
180 min	6	30 min	16.7
	5	36 min	20
	4	45 min	25
	3	60 min	33.3

* Deduct from the time available for each question, the time needed for reading *all* the questions, deciding which questions to answer, and checking your answers.

Table 2 Three ways of allocating your time in a three-hour written examination, and the possible consequences

Question	Time allocation	Marks	Time allocation	Marks	Time allocation	Marks
1	55 min	16*	55 min	16*	36 min	14
2	50 min	14	50 min	14	36 min	13
3	40 min	11	40 min	11	36 min	12
4	35 min	11	20 min	8	36 min	11
5		0	15 min	6	36 min	10*
Totals		52		55		60

* In a written answer it is difficult to score more than sixteen out of twenty for a good answer, and it is relatively easy to score half marks by attending carefully to a question that you at first thought you did not know much about.

Table 3 Tackling the question

Question time	Planning	Practical or writing	Checking
60 min	15 min	40 min	5 min

Adapted from Robert Barrass, *Study!*

16–18: RIGHTS AND DUTIES

The age of responsibility?

Do you think you are old enough to be held fully responsible for your actions? At what age do you become so? You may feel that it depends on the individual and that some people mature faster than others. But beware of this, for anyone who tells you how mature they are almost certainly isn't.

Girls in poison coffee plot

When Bradley Manor, assistant principal of Battle Creek junior high in St Paul, Minnesota, drank some coffee last week, he felt a burning sensation and instantly spat it out.

It was just as well – the coffee contained a potentially lethal dose of iodine *writes Bill Norris*.

The attempted poisoning was carried out by three 14-year-old girls called to Manor's office after being caught smoking.

One of the girls was quoted as saying: 'I liked the idea of killing.'

Two of them have admitted second degree assault and are being held at a temporary shelter. The third denies the charge and is detained in a juvenile detention centre.

From *The Times Educational Supplement*, 28 February 1986

ASSIGNMENTS ▷ ▷ ▷ ▷ ▷ ▷ ▷ ▷

1 Have you ever felt like poisoning any of your teachers? What stopped you doing so? What would you do if you found out that your best friends were planning to poison the Head of your school? Would you act differently if the plan were for a practical joke of some sort?

2 In what ways do you believe that you are more responsible now than when you were fourteen? Do you see yourself as being as responsible as your tutor?

3 Do you think people aged fourteen or sixteen or eighteen are responsible enough to decide if they should be allowed to smoke? Do you think students of the same age should be allowed to smoke in school if they choose to?

16–18: RIGHTS AND DUTIES

Laws and rules cannot distinguish between individuals if they are to be fair, or rather if they are to be seen to be fair to everyone. So there are laws that apply to everyone in the country, irrespective of their character or state of mind, just as there are rules that apply to everyone in your school or college. But laws are passed to do with many different things and there can be apparent inconsistencies among them. You may feel that school rules have similar faults.

Sixth formers when they become eighteen achieve all the legal rights and duties of adults. They can be legally convicted of a crime. The different Acts of Parliament that have been passed over the years have laid down different age limits for legal rights and duties, leading to the complicated pattern shown opposite.

ASSIGNMENTS ▷ ▷ ▷ ▷ ▷ ▷ ▷ ▷

1 Write a notice to appear at the bar of a hotel (with restaurant) saying who will or will not be served there.

2 Is there a consistent pattern to the different age limits on (a) drinking, (b) sexual activity. Compare the age limits in these two areas.

3 'Does the Minister agree that a young soldier should be sent to die for his country without having had the legal opportunity to vote, drink, marry or make a will?' Imagine that you are a civil servant asked to write a reply for your Minister to this parliamentary question. Besides writing the main reply you should anticipate possible supplementary questions and suggest suitable answers to these as well. You should, of course, justify the existing state of affairs and protect your Minister from the obligation to change anything.

16–18: RIGHTS AND DUTIES

The age(s) of responsibility in law

At ten

- you can be convicted of a criminal offence provided it is proven that you knew what you were doing.

At thirteen

- you can be employed for a limited number of hours a week.

At fourteen

- you can be convicted (if male) of a sexual or unnatural offence.
- you can be held fully responsible for a crime.
- you can play cribbage or dominoes in a room in a pub which is not a bar.

At sixteen

- you can leave school and work full time.
- you can give consent for sexual intercourse (girls only).
- you can leave home and/or marry with parent's consent.
- you can hold a licence to ride a motor-bike.
- you can enter the bar of a pub but not buy a drink unless you are buying a meal.

At seventeen

- you can hold a licence to drive most vehicles.
- you can hold a licence to possess a firearm.

At eighteen

- you have reached the age of legal majority.
- you can leave home, marry, vote, take legal actions such as making a will or suing in court.
- you can buy drinks in the bar of a pub.

At twenty-one

- you can stand as a candidate in elections.
- you can hold a licence to sell intoxicating liquor.
- you can consent in male homosexual practices, in private.

DOING THE RIGHT THING

Causing offence without meaning to

Nearly everyone has good intentions. They want other people to think well of them and they want to do the right thing. But it is sometimes difficult to tell what effect your own actions have on other people. It is all too easy to give offence without meaning to. You might be talking with your friends using the language you use with each other all the time, but which an old lady sitting nearby finds offensive. You might play around, or mix in a crowd of friends, in a way that someone outside your group finds threatening. You might be thinking of something else and so give the impression that you dislike someone who is speaking to you. We must all try to see what effect we have on others, if we are not to underestimate the importance of what we say or do.

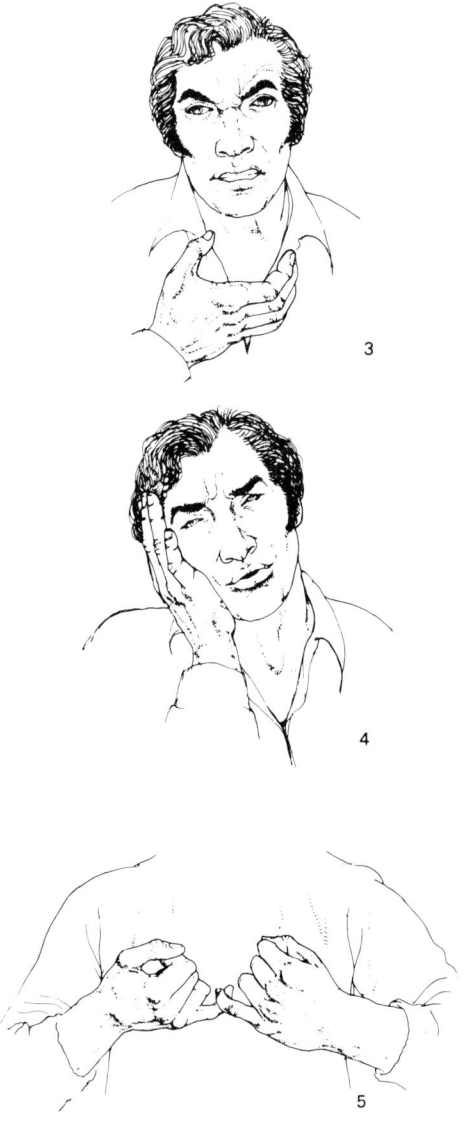

3

4

5

DOING THE RIGHT THING

6

7

8

9

Insult signals

Symbolic insults (3–9) vary greatly from culture to culture and are often meaningless outside their home range. They include: the South American Goiter sign, meaning stupidity (3), the Spanish Baby-head sign, meaning immaturity (4), the Arab Little-fingers Pull-apart movement, symbolising the end of a friendship (5), the European Long-beard gesture, meaning you are boring (6), or the Austrian version of this (7), in which the imaginary beard is stroked with the fingers. There is also the widespread and well-known 'yakity-yak' gesture (8), where the hand mimes the speaking movements of the mouth, and the 'fed-up-to-here' gesture (9).

From Desmond Morris, *Manwatching*, Jonathan Cape 1978

ASSIGNMENTS ▷ ▷ ▷ ▷ ▷ ▷ ▷ ▷

1 Find three gestures here that you might use in casual conversation with your friends, but that would give serious offence in another part of the world.

2 Try to remember an occasion when someone gave you offence without meaning to, or when you gave offence, perhaps to a teacher, without thinking that you were doing anything wrong.

3 Do students junior to you in your school or college view you any differently from the way you and your friends view each other? Do you live up to their expectations, or do you think sixth formers sometimes underestimate their importance?

DOING THE RIGHT THING

"FIFTEEN, PLEASE!"

Daily Express, 5 December 1974

Responsible behaviour?

'What an irresponsible, careless thing to do!' Has anyone said this to you or, now that you are in the sixth form, have you ever said the same thing to someone younger? Perhaps you remember that feeling when you regret that you did not think first to take more care of other people. As adults we must all take responsibility for looking after those younger or weaker than ourselves, or indeed anyone that we can help. The only problem is when we face conflicting loyalties and must choose who to look after and who not to look after. That is when we need good judgement as well as a good sense of responsibility. It would be irresponsible of us not to use all our skills and abilities to help to take care of others.

ASSIGNMENTS ▷ ▷ ▷ ▷ ▷ ▷ ▷ ▷

1 Let three of your group take on the roles of the baker, 'granny' and another customer, in the Giles cartoon above. Let each person explain his/her feelings about the 'responsibility' of 'granny's' actions. Then expand the discussion to cover the following points:
- Should shopkeepers choose who to sell to?
- Are striking bakers acting irresponsibly?
- Are conservationists and animal rights groups acting irresponsibly if they put the interests of birds or animals above those of local residents?

DOING THE RIGHT THING

How can I stop my child stealing?

'Can you help me? I am very upset: you might be able to tell me what to do about my daughter who is almost twelve years old. The trouble is she persists in stealing money from my purse and about the house, and when I tackle her about it she denies having taken anything, even when I find the money in her possession. I am so afraid that she will steal from other people, too.

'She started at a local grammar school last September, having passed the qualifying examination so I can't think that her brain is sub-normal. She also passed several ballet exams with flying colours, but now I'm afraid to let her go to ballet class in case she should steal from the other children. What am I to do? Please help me if you can. I just don't know how to deal with the situation, nor how best to punish Elizabeth. I tried stopping her pocket money for a couple of weeks, but that only seemed to make matters worse.'

ASSIGNMENTS ▷ ▷ ▷ ▷ ▷ ▷ ▷ ▷

1 Write down your own suggested explanation of why this girl may have started stealing. Do you think that she knows that she is acting irresponsibly? Why do you think she may be persisting in doing so? Compare the answers in your group.

2 Write your own answer to this letter that could be published in the 'agony column' of a monthly magazine. Write as to the mother, taking care to give your analysis and advice in the most helpful way. Compare the answers in your group. Then read the published answer on the next page.

3 Is it right to punish people? What are the forms of punishment used in your own school or college? How effective are they in teaching people to act more responsibly? What improvements could you suggest?

When a child steals

My reply:

Your daughter's stealing does not indicate any 'bad' tendency, you know. It doesn't mean she's heading for delinquency, a life of crime or anything like that. Rather, this is as much a symptom of emotional distress as a rash is a symptom of measles. She's not subnormal. She's unhappy, or disturbed, for some reason.

When a child steals it is almost always for compensation or to 'buy' goodwill or friendship. For example, a child who has an unhappy home background and feels unloved, may steal to find comfort in the possessions that she steals, or the possessions that she can buy with money she steals.

The child who feels inferior to her companions may steal simply to appear on a level with them ... not only to show that what they have she has, too, but sometimes to be able to give them sweets and suchlike in the hope that she'll be accepted.

I wonder, has your daughter started this stealing since she went to her new school? If she has, then it could be that the girls there make her feel a bit inferior for some reason. Perhaps they always seem to have more pocket money to spend, for example. Perhaps she thinks, rightly or wrongly, that their homes are smarter than her own. Maybe they have possessions that she wishes she had, and so she steals, not because she's bad, as I say, but in order to be able to keep up with them by buying things with the money she steals. Stopping her pocket money as punishment would, I'm afraid, make things worse rather than better, for if she doesn't have even her basic allowance, then her need for funds to keep up will be even more acute. Indeed, an increase if you can manage it, and feel it justified, might be a better idea.

What the girl needs is not accusations or punishment, but as much love and understanding as you can possibly give her. Try very hard to put yourself in her shoes. See if you can discover just what it is that is making her feel inferior or unhappy, what it is that's giving her this need to steal. Then deal with it sympathetically.

Choose a moment when there hasn't been a stealing episode and when you can speak to the girl lovingly, quietly and unemotionally and talk to her, not about the fact that she has stolen, but about her life and happiness in general. Try to find out, if you can, how she feels about her new school friends. Try to find out a little about their background. Perhaps having a word with her teacher might help. In confidence of course.

In any event, this is a situation to be dealt with, not by punishment and not by anger, or shock, though I do understand how you feel, but with sympathetic understanding, realising that it is, as I say, a symptom of something troubling the child, and not a result of inherent badness.

From *Woman*, 24 April 1971

SHAPING UP AS A PARENT

In 1926, a book was published by Kahlil Gibran called *The Prophet*. His advice on parenting ('Speak to us of children') is worth looking at. It includes his most memorable line for parents: 'You are the bows from which your children as living arrows are sent forth.'

How involved are your parents or guardians in your life? You probably feel that the amount of time they spend with you now is less than when you were a young child. Yet there is no denying that their influence is still one of the deepest on your life. Parenting is a job for which we all feel largely unprepared. We can read about how to do it, watch others on whom we can model (or choose not to model) our approach and try out parts of it when we are caring for children.

This unit gives you a chance to look at how society has divided up parenting into female and male roles, and to consider the fairness of this.

Working as a mum

Do you remember?

I've had a great reunion with a childhood friend. We sat for hours discussing our mothers. She started by asking 'Do you remember how your mum made all our friends birthday presents of dolls' dresses in the same material as our own party frocks?' We smiled at each other, picturing the particular doll we had proudly carried to the birthday table. 'Good grief,' she said, 'imagine having the time to make clothes for dolls.' 'Or for children in the first place,' I added. I had a vivid recollection of my mother at her sewing machine, making boxer shorts for my younger brother. Was it financial necessity that led to all those hours in her sewing corner, or was it a creative outlet for her?

So many memories picture her sitting, sewing. I remember learning for a geography test, pounding up and down the room, saying to her, 'Can you listen to me, Mum, so I can see if I've remembered it all?' And she'd look up from her stitching, smile in encouragement, and nod as I paced past her muttering boring facts. That was her place; that was women's place in her generation. She was at home, for us, her family.

'Imagine too,' my friend continued, 'even getting one of the girls into a party frock!' She has three daughters, ranging from eleven to two years old. 'I took the day off work for Susie's birthday (she's the two-year-old), and we went to the park together in the morning, and had six little friends to lunch. It was strange being the only mum there, though. All the other children came with nannies or childminders. They all knew each other well of course . . .'

'Do you remember the ice cream sodas your mum used to produce at parties?' I had another sudden mental image. 'Ooh,' she grinned, 'in those green glasses. But Susie's a bit young for fizzy drinks . . .'

SHAPING UP AS A PARENT

ASSIGNMENTS ▷ ▷ ▷ ▷ ▷ ▷ ▷ ▷

1 What part does your mother play in the memories of your childhood? Discuss with a friend.

2 Do you wish she did not or had not worked? Can you say why?

3 Would you expect to work once you have children?

4 Why are more women with children working now than in the past?

5 How can a working parent/guardian make the most of family life?

6 Draw up a family agreement that you could realistically put to your family so that your family life is enhanced.

Working as a dad

Look at the newspaper article opposite and then do the following assignments.

ASSIGNMENTS ▷ ▷ ▷ ▷ ▷ ▷ ▷ ▷

1 What do you think of the following points from the article?

'And even men who believe they share childcare and housework do less than they think.'

'. . . belief that the mother is the best person to care for her children . . .'.

2 Is a father's role more difficult than a mother's?

3 What do you think should be your parents'/guardians' roles towards you this year? How can you help them to achieve this?

Does he deserve it?

Father's Day is on Sunday: Lee Rodwell asks if the modern British father merits recognition

Greetings card manufacturers expect to sell about 20 million cards in celebration of Father's Day and the market, which is now fast-growing, is worth £10 million to them . . . .

Is this simply the result of a successful marketing campaign, or do we really believe that the modern father's contribution to family life deserves recognition? The American woman who, in 1910, launched the campaign for a special day for fathers had no doubts. Mrs John Bruce Dodd apparently said: 'Either we honour both of our parents, mother *and* father or we should desist from honouring either one.'

Mrs JBD had reason to be on the side of fathers – her own raised a family of six single-handed after his wife died. Yet few fathers put so much time and effort into parenting. Indeed, evidence from a variety of sources shows that the majority of fathers still regard their main role as a parent to be a breadwinner – whether their own wives work or not. And even men who believe they share childcare and housework do less than they think.

Dr Andrew Stanway, a psychosexual and marital counsellor, and author of *A Woman's Guide to Men and Sex*, acknowledges the fact that fathers tend to back away from the day-to-day business of childcare.

Dad isn't in the picture: the drawing used in British Telecom's advertising

'Bringing up children is a long-term affair and the rewards are hard to define,' he says. 'To most men this is a difficult pill to swallow, because everything else in their lives is geared to producing results on a day-by-day or month-by-month basis. This kind of achievement-centred life is hard to apply to children especially when they are young.'

Stanway admits that men encourage our culture's underlying belief that the mother is the best person to care for her children, but he also feels that many fathers would do more if their wives did not 'sabotage' their efforts. 'Many women, however unconsciously, dissuade their men from having a meaningful part to play with the children because it is the only role they, the wives, have that is of value to *them*. Such women put their men down as fathers, perhaps even telling them how inept they are, often as a joke, but the damage is done and the man feels inadequate as a father.'

He dislikes the idea of one day a year being dubbed Father's Day – 'Fathers need to be loved all the time, just as mothers do' – but given that the day is recognized by some, he feels fathers could do more to be worthy of their gifts and cards by spending more time simply being with their children.

From *The Times*, 17 June 1988

SHAPING UP AS A PARENT

Parental responsibilities

Flowers ease the pain for mother who reported son

By A J McIlroy

A BOUQUET from anonymous well-wishers has 'doubly convinced' Mrs Noreen Falk that she did the right thing by informing police when she found a small amount of cannabis in her 19-year-old son's bedroom.

'The flowers were on the seat of my car with a card and the message "From concerned members of the public" saying that I had taken the right decision,' she said yesterday.

She said the gesture had helped ease the pain of knowing that her action had led to her son, Andrew, being fined and losing his job.

Even the fact that he was no longer speaking to her had not weakened her resolve.

'The flowers are part of a tremendous response I have had from people who agree absolutely with my stand. They all say I was right in deciding that my son would listen to the police more than he would to me.

'It seems that my action in reporting it to the police has struck a chord.

'The response from the public has been so reassuring. And when I returned to my car and found the flowers and that message I realised just how much parents everywhere are worried about getting their children to listen and realise the dangers of drugs.

Mrs Falk, 45, who lives with her son and two younger children in Maidenhead, Berks, found the drug on the window ledge of her son's bedroom.

Andrew Falk was fined £80 by the town's magistrates, who were told that he had been smoking cannabis since December.

In an interview yesterday, he said he planned to leave home and was no longer speaking to his mother.

'I have got nothing to say to her,' he said, at his mother's house. 'I think she was wrong to go to the police.

'She should have talked to me first and then, if she had still wanted to, I would have gone to the police with her. This hasn't done me any good at all because now I have a criminal record.'

Told of her son's comments, Mrs Falk said: 'I was very much aware, like other parents, that I have a responsibility to my children. Parents are being told they should be responsible for their children's actions.'

From the *Daily Telegraph*, 20 June 1988

ASSIGNMENTS ▷ ▷ ▷ ▷ ▷ ▷ ▷ ▷

1 In pairs, work out the issues that are revealed by this event.

2 Join up with another pair and put one of you in the 'hot seat' as Mrs Falk, and another as Andrew. Interview the character about how she/he felt about the incident.

3 In the full group, discuss whether you agree with Mrs Falk's action.

4 Role-play in the groups of four a scene in which Mrs Falk and Andrew are reunited (a year?) later.

EARNING AND SPENDING

Imagine that you had no one to support you – no family, no friends, no social security. You would still need to spend money to survive, on food, drink, clothing, accommodation, at the least. You would have to find money to pay for all this spending; if you were desperate you might beg, borrow or steal, but more likely you would find work to earn your living.

This is the situation you are likely to find yourself in when you finish full-time studying. You will be earning your own income at work, and spending on the goods and services you buy. This is likely to be very different from your present way of life, where you probably rely on other people's work to earn the money to keep you, and where you live off other people's spending as well as some of your own.

ASSIGNMENTS ▷ ▷ ▷ ▷ ▷ ▷ ▷ ▷

1 Look at the graph below. Which categories of spending by families, as a proportion of total spending:

(a) rise with income?
(b) fall as income rises?
(c) stay much the same?

Suggest reasons for these differences.

2 Estimate the maximum amounts of money that might be saved up over a year towards a foreign holiday by the richest and poorest family shown here. Compare the sums spent on 'alcohol' per week by the same two families. Is it fairer to compare in relative (percentage) or absolute (money totals) terms?

3 Estimate your personal income and spending per week in terms of the same categories of spending. Which standard categories do not apply to you and why not?

Family budgets
Average family spending in three income bands

1 Income before deducting tax, NI contributions etc.
2 Includes interest on mortgage but not mortgage repayments
3 Includes telephone, postage and miscellaneous
4 Covers tax, NI, life insurance, savings, investments and mortgage repayments

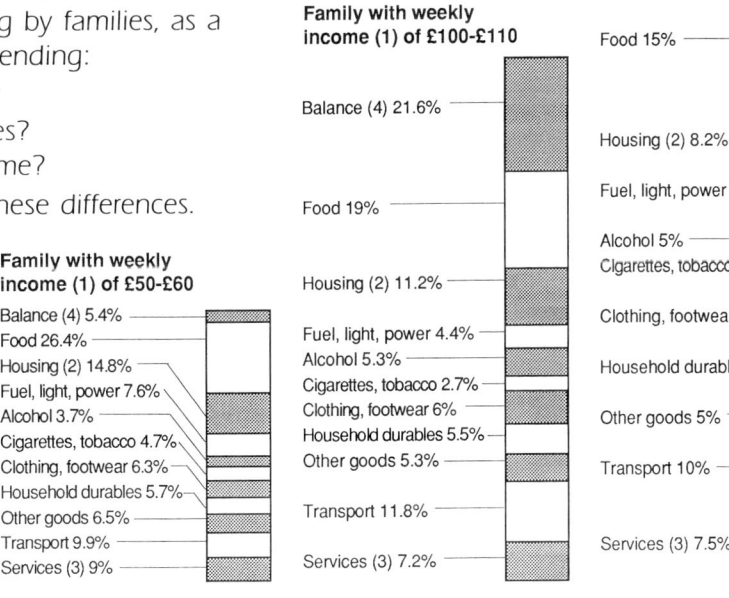

Family with weekly income (1) of £150-£200

Balance (4) 32.6%
Food 15%
Housing (2) 8.2%
Fuel, light, power 3%
Alcohol 5%
Cigarettes, tobacco 2.2%
Clothing, footwear 6.5%
Household durables 5%
Other goods 5%
Transport 10%
Services (3) 7.5%

Family with weekly income (1) of £100-£110

Balance (4) 21.6%
Food 19%
Housing (2) 11.2%
Fuel, light, power 4.4%
Alcohol 5.3%
Cigarettes, tobacco 2.7%
Clothing, footwear 6%
Household durables 5.5%
Other goods 5.3%
Transport 11.8%
Services (3) 7.2%

Family with weekly income (1) of £50-£60

Balance (4) 5.4%
Food 26.4%
Housing (2) 14.8%
Fuel, light, power 7.6%
Alcohol 3.7%
Cigarettes, tobacco 4.7%
Clothing, footwear 6.3%
Household durables 5.7%
Other goods 6.5%
Transport 9.9%
Services (3) 9%

From *The Which? Book of Money*, Consumers' Association, p. 161

ORGANISE YOUR MONEY

How much money have you got and how well do you look after it? One good measure of how well you organise your money is to see if you can answer the assignments opposite. Your cash may be scattered in different pockets so you do not know how much you have, you may just spend it as soon as you get it without planning how. The figures that follow show how young people aged up to seventeen receive and spend their money. Obviously values change over the years because of inflation and increasing prosperity, but relative values are not much changed by this. See how you fit in with the average picture.

The young, and their money

Where the money comes from

Ages 11-17	£m
Pocket money	466.56
Regular job	1846.99
Errands	250.10
Money from parents for specific purposes	296.04
Occasional money/ gifts from relatives	262.25
Total for age group	3121.94

Carrick James Market Research National Survey 1985

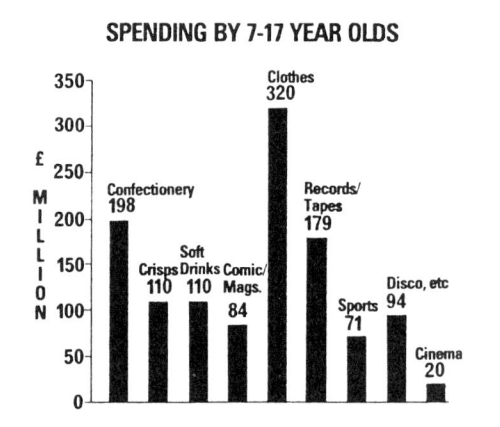

SPENDING BY 7-17 YEAR OLDS

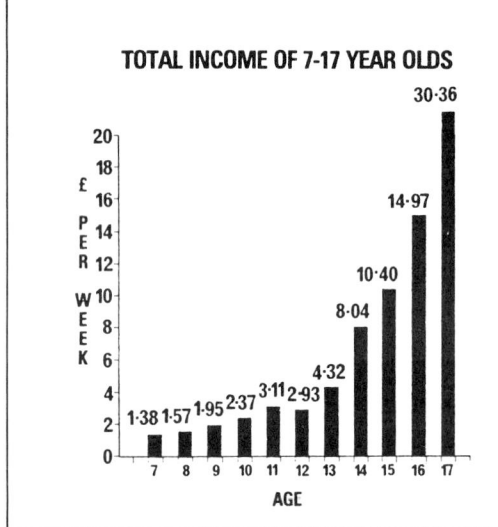

TOTAL INCOME OF 7-17 YEAR OLDS

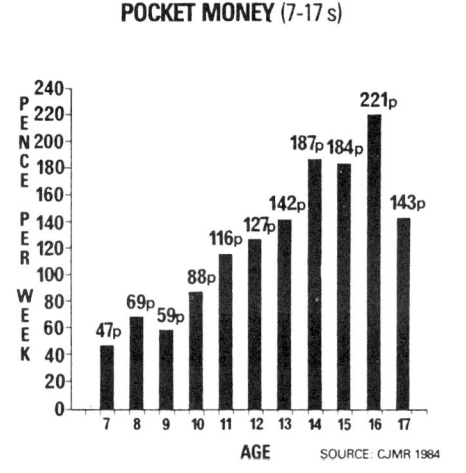

POCKET MONEY (7-17 s)

SOURCE: CJMR 1984

From *Money Care*, published by the National Westminster Bank, 1986

ORGANISE YOUR MONEY

ASSIGNMENTS ▷ ▷ ▷ ▷ ▷ ▷ ▷ ▷

1 On average, what share of young people's income do they earn for themselves? Why do you think 'pocket money' allowances fall after sixteen? Do you have an allowance and has it fallen recently?

2 What proportion of young people's spending is on durable goods? Do you think that most young people tend to spend their money wastefully? How can you decide what is wasteful or sensible spending?

3 To what extent do young people show increasing independence in their use of money as they grow older? Do you see your money as a source of independence?

How much do you save each week, and when you save is it because you forgot to spend or because you are saving up to buy something? Money can work for you if you know how to organise it. Bank and building society accounts help you to look after your money, to carry it with you in a safer way, and to earn interest while you save it. But banks and building societies want your money so that they can organise it as well, to lend out to their customers on overdraft, say, or mortgage. It pays to consider the alternatives open to you – to spend all your cash as you get it, or to save some and earn extra in interest for future spending, or to borrow and pay a rate of interest so that you get what you want without having to wait and save up. Spending and saving are tied closely together.

ORGANISE YOUR MONEY

The cost of children

The figure shows what a family spends on children of different ages out of each £ of income they take home. As the child grows up, the number of pence in the £ spent on him or her rises – to 26p for a child in the 16–17 age group.

These figures are based on families with incomes between two-thirds and twice the national average – families with very low incomes are likely to spend a higher proportion of their incomes on supporting their children. And families with above-average incomes might well wish to spend more on their children – sending them to private school, or training them in more expensive sports like skiing or flying.

On average, about 18p of each £ spent by a family with one child goes on supporting the child up to the age of 18. For a family with two children the figure rises to 28p of each £.

ASSIGNMENTS ▷ ▷ ▷ ▷ ▷ ▷ ▷ ▷

1 Why do you think spending differs for different ages of children, and for 'first' or 'second' children?

2 Estimate what you will have cost your parents as a share of their income, on the average values shown, so far.

3 Design a poster, or write a radio commercial or some other advertisement, that aims to 'sell' to parents the reasons why they should, or should not, 'support their children'.

How much is spent on a child?

Pence in the pound from income:

How much is spent on two children?

Pence in the pound from income:

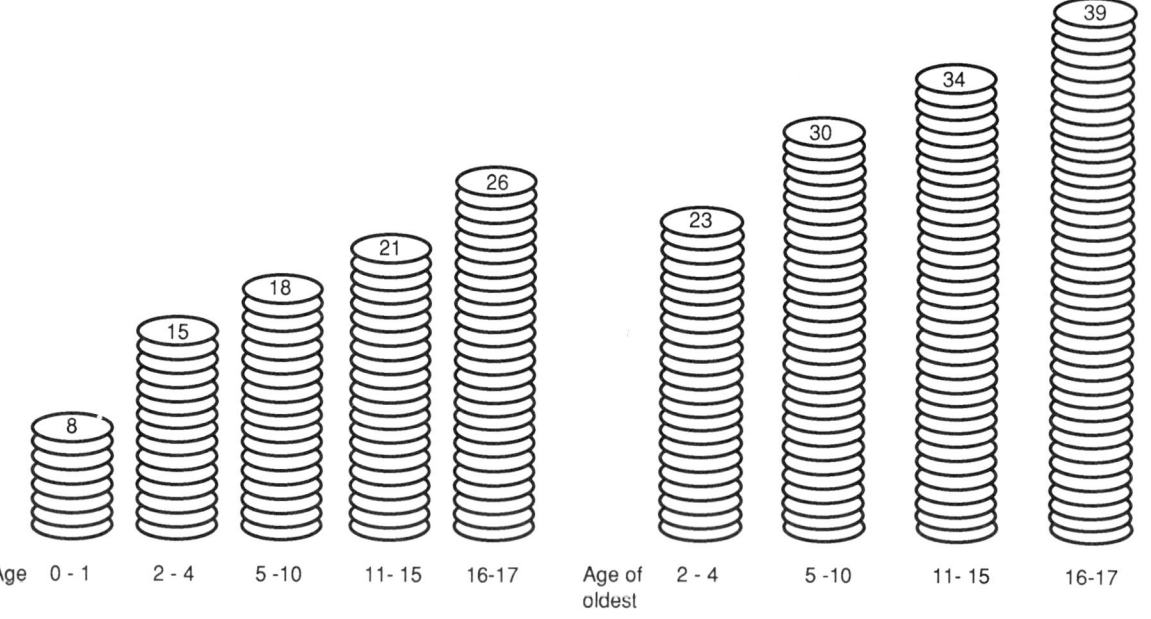

One child: Age 0-1: 8; 2-4: 15; 5-10: 18; 11-15: 21; 16-17: 26

Two children (Age of oldest): 2-4: 23; 5-10: 30; 11-15: 34; 16-17: 39

Based on a graph in *The Which? Book of Money*, Consumers' Association, p. 153

CONSUMER SKILLS

Getting value for money

Are you good at spending money? Any fool can be quickly parted from his or her cash, but we have all bought things from time to time that we decide later were a waste of money. It takes a certain amount of skill to find the best buy and to make sure that your money is well spent. You must make up your own mind. Think through what different choices have to offer, and weigh up the value for money offered by each.

ASSIGNMENTS ▷ ▷ ▷ ▷ ▷ ▷ ▷ ▷

1 Think of something you wanted to have but you did not have enough money; something you shopped around for in order to find the best buy; and something you wanted at almost any price. Why do you think your approach to these three purchases differed?

2 Have you ever bought anything that became a disappointing waste of money – a particular record, or a computer, or some clothing you would never dare wear? Why do you think you did buy it, and how could you avoid making the same mistake again?

3 Give an example of an advertisement that purely informs and another that persuades people to buy.

ASSIGNMENTS ▷ ▷ ▷ ▷ ▷ ▷ ▷ ▷

Turn to page 94 and read the four cases. Act as a lawyer giving legal advice on each of them. Explain the principles involved in layman's terms, state your client's rights in the matter, and give advice on his next course of action. Prepare, then present your answers in groups. Research as necessary from your local library.

1 **'The coach didn't go'** Notice that goods and services, when sold, must be 'of merchantable quality', 'as described' and 'fit for the purpose for which sold'. Consider also the significance of possible conditions (written on tickets etc.) excluding companies from responsibility for unforeseen errors.

2 **'Suing a petrol station'** Notice the significance of licensing and safety regulations imposed by the Trading Standards Department and the Fire Brigade, as well as the legal relationship between seller and buyer.

3 **'When to insist on a cash refund'** Notice that retailers are obliged to sell 'merchantable' goods to customers and failing that, customers have the right to their money back. Alternatively customers may agree with the retailer to a replacement or a credit note instead.

4 **'The stolen badger'** Notice the importance of 'title' to legal ownership and the ways it can be transferred from one person to another.

CONSUMER SKILLS

What are your rights as a consumer?

The coach didn't go
Mr Woollard, Milford Haven
On 22 September, my wife and I travelled to London by coach from Milford Haven on a National Travel ticket with a confirmed return date of 1 October.

When we arrived at Victoria for the return journey, we were informed that the service had been withdrawn the previous Sunday, owing to an industrial dispute. No alternative transport had been laid on. We had to return home by British Rail at an additional cost of £19.76.

Suing a petrol station
Mr Rockell, Slough
At a self-service petrol station, I filled up with petrol and found that the cut-off on the pump failed to work. My shoes and trousers were soaked, the car was stained down the side and a substantial pool of petrol was spilt on to the forecourt.

The garage staff were totally unconcerned and their remarks indicated that they were already aware of the fault. No reduction was allowed on the total price shown on the pump; I had to send my trousers for dry cleaning, and the car had to be washed.

When to insist on a cash refund
Mr Browning, Dover
I bought a tape recorder but, because it was faulty, returned it to the shop at the first possible opportunity. The shop accepted that it was faulty – but wasn't able to supply a replacement, and gave me a credit note.

Later, from another shop, I bought a stereo receiver including a tape deck – so no longer had any need for the original tape recorder. I returned to the first shop and asked for a refund on the credit note, but the shop refused.

Who owns the stolen badger?
Mr Rees, Bristol
A badger mounted in a glass case disappeared from the biology laboratory of a college to which I had loaned it. Three months later, two students saw the badger for sale in an antique shop in Bristol. After confirming this, but not contacting the dealer, I set out the facts in a letter to the Bristol Police and delivered it the following morning.

On the following Thursday I was telephoned by the police and told that the dealer did not dispute any of the facts, but that he had bought the badger in good faith and the only way I could regain possession was by negotiating for its purchase.

I have seen the dealer concerned who confirms that he is protected by law, but is prepared to sell it back to me for the £20 he paid for it.

From 'What are your rights as a consumer?', in *Which?*, Consumers' Association

CONSUMER SKILLS

How to put things right

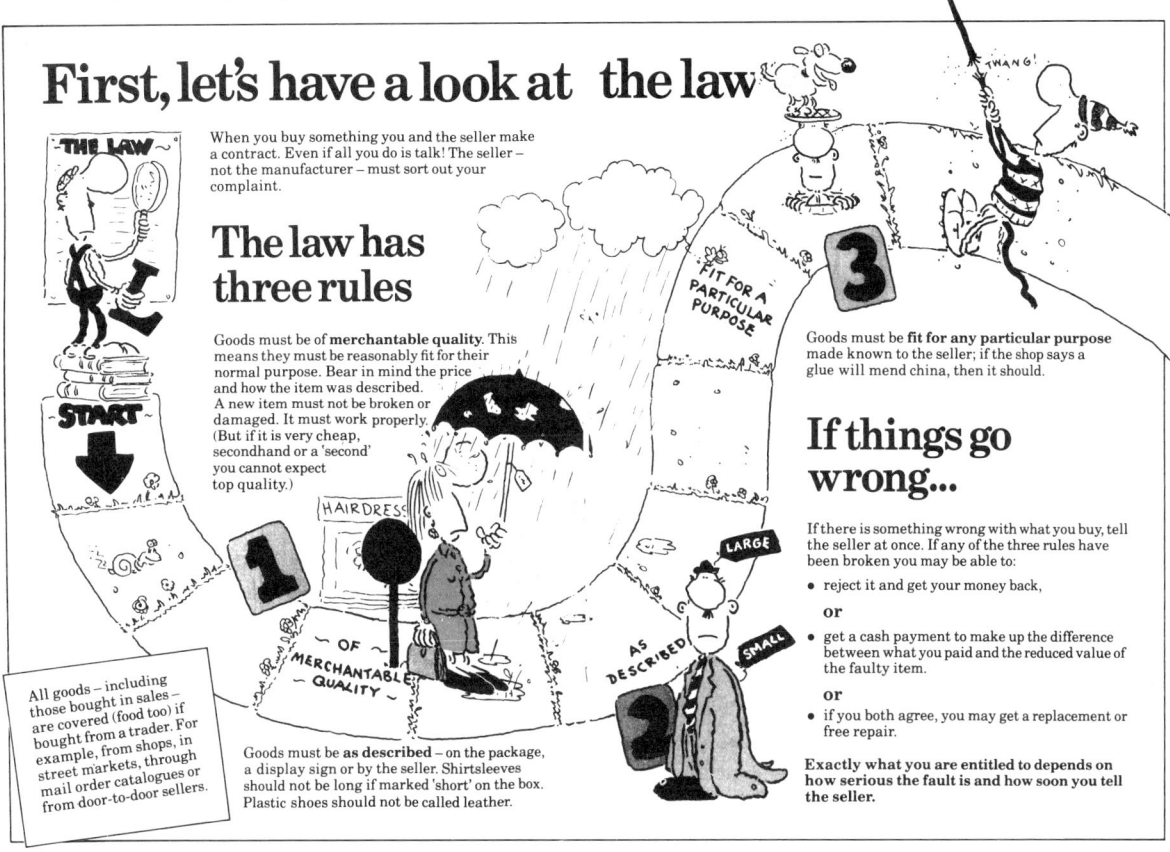

First, let's have a look at the law

THE LAW

START

When you buy something you and the seller make a contract. Even if all you do is talk! The seller – not the manufacturer – must sort out your complaint.

The law has three rules

Goods must be of **merchantable quality**. This means they must be reasonably fit for their normal purpose. Bear in mind the price and how the item was described. A new item must not be broken or damaged. It must work properly. (But if it is very cheap, secondhand or a 'second' you cannot expect top quality.)

HAIRDRESS

1 OF MERCHANTABLE QUALITY

All goods – including those bought in sales – are covered (food too) if bought from a trader. For example, from shops, in street markets, through mail order catalogues or from door-to-door sellers.

Goods must be **as described** – on the package, a display sign or by the seller. Shirtsleeves should not be long if marked 'short' on the box. Plastic shoes should not be called leather.

2 AS DESCRIBED

LARGE SMALL

FIT FOR A PARTICULAR PURPOSE

3

Goods must be **fit for any particular purpose** made known to the seller; if the shop says a glue will mend china, then it should.

If things go wrong...

If there is something wrong with what you buy, tell the seller at once. If any of the three rules have been broken you may be able to:

- reject it and get your money back,

  or

- get a cash payment to make up the difference between what you paid and the reduced value of the faulty item.

  or

- if you both agree, you may get a replacement or free repair.

Exactly what you are entitled to depends on how serious the fault is and how soon you tell the seller.

From an Office of Fair Trading pamphlet, HMSO, 1980

ASSIGNMENTS ▷ ▷ ▷ ▷ ▷ ▷ ▷ ▷

1 Let three of your group take roles as customer, shop assistant and manager. The customer returns to the shop where he or she bought some shoes last month, one of which has now broken. The rest of the group should judge how well the customer 'complains', how well the customer and retailer know their rights and responsibilities, and how far they go in upholding them.

2 Have any of your group had difficulties with faulty goods or services? What did they do about it, was this satisfactory, what more could have been done?

3 Write a letter 'complaining' about an unsatisfactory product or service you have bought. State all the relevant information and ask for your money back. Make it clear that you know your rights as a customer, and how to enforce them.

HEALTH AND DIET

Choosing healthy food

Shown on this page are two standard menus such as you might eat tonight when you get home. The meal on the left is made up of good British favourites – red meats, salt, refined sugars, and saturated fats. In terms of good taste its virtues may be debatable. In terms of good health it is a disaster. It is not merely fattening and non-nutritious, it is, as a life-time diet, damaging to your heart and kidneys. Probably the greatest single step to cut the number of premature deaths due to cardiovascular diseases would be to switch the British population over to eating meals like the one on the right. This offers good nourishment in terms of fibre, vitamins, minerals, protein and essential fats. It avoids the added sugars, salt and saturated fats that are so damaging. It may even taste better!

Which would you choose?

Which one of the two meals shown most resembles a meal you ate yesterday? Compare within your group to put together a composite menu: that is the meal the majority had yesterday. What does this tell you?

ASSIGNMENTS ▷ ▷ ▷ ▷ ▷ ▷ ▷ ▷

1 Choose one of the two meals shown. Check in your Tutor Group to see how everyone chooses. What would people add or take away if they could change one course?

2 How much do you think about what you eat or drink? How often do you prepare your own meals? Which is most important: convenience, taste, or good health?

3 Prepare a menu of your favourite food and drink. Compare it with others in the group.

Beefburgers
Salted chips
Ketchup
White bread and butter with jam
Coke
Ice-cream and Cream 'delight'
Coffee with sugar and cream

Chicken pieces
Jacket potatoes
Brown bread and cheese
Fruit juice
Two apples
Coffee with skimmed milk

THE FOOD SCANDAL

Like the rest of us, children on average consume around one-fifth of their calories in the form of processed, 'refined' sugars. A popular classroom exercise conducted by knowledgeable teachers nowadays, as seen on television, is to show children the amount of sugars they eat (in the form of confectionery, soft drinks, cakes, biscuits, and so forth) by measuring it out by the spoonfuls. The children are amazed. Their parents are outraged.

People are surprised to learn that the British population consumes about 40 per cent of total calories in the form of fat, and 20 per cent as processed sugars. And 'not me' they say. 'I've stopped taking sugar in coffee and trim the fat off my meat'. But there is more – much more – fat and sugars in food than meets the eye. Milk, for example. Of silver top milk, 52 per cent of calories is fat. And here are some other figures for fat. Cheddar cheese: 71 per cent. Full fat yoghurt: same as milk, 52 per cent. Bacon, 60–80 per cent; red meat, 55–75 per cent: that extra 20 per cent, the difference between 60 and 80, or 55 and 75, is the fat you trim off. Sausages, 70 per cent. Butter or margarine, 100 per cent. What about 'low-fat' spreads like Gold or Outline? They are margarine with added water, together with something like gelatine to stick it together so it looks like margarine rather than an oil slick:

percentage of calories that are fat, still 100.

What about sugars? If you measure the percentage of the weight of a soft drink like Coca Cola composed of sugars, the result sounds almost reassuring: 10. But the other 90 per cent is water, so, percentage of calories in Coca Cola in the form of sugars: 100. The lot. Other figures for sugars? All-Bran: 22. Ice-cream: 55. Sweetened orange juice: 63; and that does not include the sugars from the orange itself. Canned fruit in syrup: 60–80 per cent. Baked beans: 31 per cent calories added sugars. Oh, and tomato ketchup: 94 per cent of calories added sugars.

There are then the foods which are 'sweet fat', containing saturated fats made palatable by added sugars. Ice-cream again: 32 per cent fat, making a total of 87 per cent fat and sugars together. Fruit-flavoured yoghurt: 63 per cent total fat and added sugars. Digestive biscuits: with chocolate, 65 per cent; plain, 53 per cent. And what about the favourite British soup, cream of tomato? That's 89 per cent of energy supplied by fat and sugars, which puts it up close to the Mars Bar league. Much of the food most commonly eaten in Britain has only marginally more nourishment in it than candy.

Public health is not a party political issue. Farmers, miners, and politicians, all have an equal

interest in avoiding premature death. The view of the Conservative Government is that citizens should be free to make their own choices, even when such choices may kill them, as with smoking.

But when you buy a packet of cigarettes, you have some idea of what you might be letting yourself in for. Apart from the government health warning, there is another label (which may or may not be a useful guide) saying HIGH or MEDIUM or LOW TAR. The unhealthy choice to smoke is an informed choice. Choice requires information.

There are those who state, from a position suggesting authority, that fat, sugar and salt, in the quantities we now consume them in Britain today, are harmless to health. As far as I know these people are all employed, paid by or associated with the food industry, full time or as consultants. There may be others whose connection with the industry is limited to working for a university department whose buildings and research are partly funded by the industry.

For the rest of us, informed choice about food means explicit food labelling. And this means not only ingredient labelling, but nutritional labelling. We have a right to know just how much fat, saturated fat, sugars, salt and fibre a food contains.

From Geoffrey Cannon in *The Times*, 13 June 1984

ASSIGNMENTS ▷ ▷ ▷ ▷ ▷ ▷ ▷ ▷

1 Choose two of your group to act as representatives of the British Food Industry and two to act as members of a 'healthy eating' pressure group. Hold a press conference with each pair so that the rest of the group can act as journalists asking questions about the views and policies of each. Try to use the material in the article as a basis for further questions.

2 The Common Agricultural Policy of the European Community spends two thirds of the Community's budget and supports production of dairy products, sugar and wine especially heavily. What are the reasons for such subsidies? What is their effect on European diet?

3 Should people be allowed to 'eat whatever they like'? Are you satisfied with your own diet, and with what you know about it? With a friend plan a week's menu.

HEALTH AND ACTIVITY

How much time have you spent on exercise this week? In an age apparently obsessed by 'keeping fit' it is astonishing that a lot of our leisure time is spent sitting in front of the television.

And does being fit make any difference to our appearance and self image? 'Fat' is a highly subjective word. At the National Science Museum, an exhibition about cooking through the ages had three mirrors for visitors to walk past. Two distorted the viewer's reflection. The majority of women had to be persuaded that the enlarged view of themselves was *not* their real selves.

Body image questionnaire

Rate yourself on each of the statements below, rating 0 if it is never applicable, 1 if it is occasionally true for you, 2 for sometimes and 3 for frequently.

I dislike seeing myself in mirrors   0 1 2 3

Shopping for clothes can be uncomfortable because it makes me more aware of my size and shape   0 1 2 3

I think my body is ugly   0 1 2 3

I avoid exercising in public because of my appearance   0 1 2 3

I feel embarrassed about my appearance in front of someone of the opposite sex   0 1 2 3

Certain parts of my body are OK, but the overall effect is not   0 1 2 3

I'm ashamed to be seen in public in a bikini, swimsuit or shorts   0 1 2 3

I compare myself with other people to see if they are fatter than I am   0 1 2 3

I feel that other people must think my body is unattractive   0 1 2 3

I may joke about my appearance but I'm very sensitive if other people remark on it   0 1 2 3

I feel guilty about my size   0 1 2 3

I don't like having my photograph taken   0 1 2 3

I spend a lot of time thinking about my appearance   0 1 2 3

If I were slimmer I think I would be more attractive to the opposite sex   0 1 2 3

When things are going well for me, I feel less dissatisfied with my body   0 1 2 3

What your score means: If you scored under 15, you are fortunate in having a good body image and a high level of self-confidence. A score of 16 to 30 indicates a moderate dissatisfaction with your body and definite scope for improvement. If you scored more than 30, your body image is poor and you should take active steps to improve it.

(Adapted from 'Taking Charge of Your Weight and Wellbeing' by Dr Joyce Nash)

From O. Gillie and S. Raby, *The Sunday Times ABC Diet and Body Plan*, Hutchinson, 1984

HEALTH AND ACTIVITY

ASSIGNMENTS ▷ ▷ ▷ ▷ ▷ ▷ ▷ ▷

1 How and why do you think your answers to the Body Image questionnaire might have changed over the last three or four years? Discuss the same questionnaire with your tutor and parent/guardian and see if their age difference makes them feel differently from you.

2 What do you think it means to 'keep in shape'? Do you think in those terms, or take exercise to do so? How could you expect to keep in shape in future?

3 Does body shape matter to the opposite sex? Should it matter? You might like to discuss the point 'Fat is a feminist issue'.

4 Try the Harvard Step Test.

The Harvard Step Test

Using a high bench or a similar object, such as steps of a stairway (ranging from 12 to 20 inches in height), step up and down 30 times a minute for 5 minutes, unless you must stop sooner because of exhaustion. Afterwards, immediately sit on a chair. After 1 minute, count your pulse for $\frac{1}{2}$ minute; after 2 minutes, count it again for $\frac{1}{2}$ minute; and after 3 minutes, again for $\frac{1}{2}$ minute.

Then calculate your Physical Efficiency Index (PEI) as follows:

$$PEI = \frac{\text{duration of exercise in seconds} \times 100}{\text{sum of pulse counts in recovery} \times 2}$$

So, if a person exercised the full 5 minutes (300 seconds) and his recovery pulse rates were 80, 60, and 40 his formula would show:

$$PEI = \frac{300 \times 100}{180 \times 2} = 83$$

A score of 83 would be an exceptionally high PEI for anyone over 30. The scale of fitness with this test is roughly as follows:

Interpretation of PEI

SCORE		AGE	
	Under 30	*30–50*	*Over 50*
90	excellent		
80–89	good	excellent	
65–79	high average	good	excellent
55–64	low average	average	good
55	poor	poor	poor

Adapted from Dr William Guild, *How to Keep Fit and Enjoy It*, New York: Harper & Row, 1962

A SPORTING CHANCE

Fitness and health have become national obsessions, spawning new gyms and exercise studios all over the country. Yet despite this revolution, attitudes towards physical exercise within our schools have remained largely unchanged. PE lessons still frequently concentrate on traditional team games which cater for a sporty elite at the expense of the also–ran majority and disenchanted non-starters.

Enlightened PE teachers, particularly in inner cities are trying to motivate and interest children with all-embracing programmes that will prepare them for the increased leisure of the future. But many diehard drill sergeants still train their pupils for a rerun of the Battle of the Somme, using the faint hearted as foils for their ready wit and putting them off sport for life. Failure on a sports field can be uniquely mortifying and many children deliberately forget their kit or invent bogus injuries rather than venture forth.

Resisting change

Any attempt to rethink the traditional policy and provide a broader range of physical activities that would also appeal to non-competitive or less talented pupils provokes heated opposition. *The Daily Mail* recently castigated the 'radical educationalists' for killing off team sports and abandoning 'our sporting heritage', although Stuart Biddle, secretary of the Psychology Section of the British Association of Sports Sciences, points out that for many children school sport is sheer purgatory and only about five per cent ever make the school team anyway. 'We are doing our children a gross disservice if we continue to produce a generally unfit nation that thinks exercise means competitive sport, from which 95 per cent have decided to opt out.'

American research has shown that while competition benefited a small group of children, many found that it lowered their self-esteem and caused excessive anxiety, he says. 'We don't need PE teachers who are simply glorified sports coaches teaching a small number of games in which most children will never participate again. School sport should be applicable for a lifetime.'

'Fortunately, there is a move in some areas towards taking the individual first, not the sport, encouraging as much participation as possible and emphasising effort rather than ability.' He adds, 'Critics claim that we have "gone soft" and "that's why we don't win the World Cup". But coaching a national team is one thing, children's needs are different.

'A lot of young girls are concerned about improving their shape. Yet they often think that exercise means only team games and so they dodge class and compensate with ill-advised crash diets. If they experience fitness instruction, however, it is surprising how many antagonistic girls become extremely receptive.'

Innovative scheme

Shirley Jeffray joined Coventry City Council eight years ago as an educational advisor and found PE teachers dissatisfied with the curriculum, particularly for girls over 14.

She set up a study group, which produced curriculum guidelines entitled 'Look good, feel fit'. 'We are looking at PE as an important part of children's personal development,' she says. 'PE has 10 per cent of the curriculum and because we are concerned with the whole person, we work with colleagues in science and home economics.'

The authority won a three year grant from the Sports Council, which wants to encourage children to continue with sport after leaving school. Coventry's 'Active Lifestyle' project, which Shirley Jeffray laughingly admits 'sounds a bit like dog food', does just that.

Four very different secondary schools are being monitored, with other city schools also involved in the scheme to a lesser extent. Pupils are given 'leisure experience'. They are taken to sports and rackets centres and local clubs and taught how to use the facilities. The PE curriculum is also tailored to fit what is available out of school and a survey of some 1500 pupils has identified their likes and dislikes. A health and fitness programme has been introduced and there is a foundation course of gymnastics, swimming, dance, outdoor pursuits and traditional sports for first and second year pupils, before they choose from a wide variety of options at 14.

Jayne Wilson, head of PE, music and drama at one of the monitored schools, outlines the results of the pupils' survey. Badminton was favourite in three schools and second to football in an all-boys school. The girls also enjoyed football and have their own team in one school. Rugby was either loved or hated. Volleyball, basketball and netball were popular, along with 'jazzercise'. Dance was both liked and disliked, and cross-country and hockey were big aversions.

Consequently cross-country is no longer a filler on wet afternoons. PE teachers have switched to working indoors on individual pupils' fitness plans, in which children keep a record of their own stamina exercises and pulse rates.

Healthy competition

'Our standards have not dropped, teams are still successful in intercounty events,' says Jayne Wilson. 'My school had an England netball player last year. We cream off good kids to the teams because we must cater for them too.' But provision is made for the rest, with lessons in personal fitness, health, hygiene, beauty and make-up swelling the variety of physical education. In one school there is even an obesity group, taught on its own and given extra PE, much as slow learners get remedial help. They no longer feel like large, clumsy freaks in the class and they 'really do try twice as hard'.

Nevertheless, while providing sport for all we must also nurture the best. In the end, these are the ones most likely to fire children's imagination. How many more potential sporting aces could be encouraged if they were offered a much wider and more flexible range of physical activities from the start?

ASSIGNMENTS ▷ ▷ ▷ ▷ ▷ ▷ ▷ ▷

1 Write a school assessment of your own performance at PE and games (a) when you were fourteen, (b) now. Then write a report of the PE and games curriculum as it affects you in your own school or college.

2 Which sports and physical activities do you most enjoy (a) playing, (b) watching? Are you involved with these in your school or college? What do you expect to continue an active interest in after you leave the sixth form? Where will you play? What physical activity do your parents/guardians and their friends keep up now? Why do you think Britain does not produce more world champions?

3 In groups devise a programme that could be adopted in your own school or college to interest and involve all students in physical exercise, such that they might keep up their interest in exercise in later life. In turn, present your proposals to the rest of the group.

From P. Mowbray, *Good Housekeeping*, April 1986

BE SAFE, NOT SORRY

Heart disease

Heart attacks, strokes and other blood system diseases are the main cause of death for men over thirty-four and second only to cancer for women over thirty-four. But the risks of heart disease can be made more or less depending on your lifestyle. As a teenager you may be young, active and fit enough to keep these risks low, but what happens later?

Heart risk

Study each risk factor in the chart opposite then find the item applicable to you. Add up your total score as an estimate of your risk. Score:

  6–11   risk well below average
 12–17   risk below average
 18–24   risk generally average
 25–31   risk moderate
 32–40   risk at a dangerous level
 41–60   danger urgent – see your doctor.

ASSIGNMENTS ▷ ▷ ▷ ▷ ▷ ▷ ▷ ▷

1 Use the chart to estimate the degree of risk that your physique and lifestyle imposes on you now, and try to predict the future value for the way of life you expect to lead when you are over forty.

2 Which of the coronary risk factors shown in the chart would you expect to be related to one another, and why?

3 Write a memorandum as a medical adviser to a government minister suggesting ways to reduce the rate of heart disease in society.

BE SAFE, NOT SORRY

Age	10 to 20	21 to 30	31 to 40	41 to 50	51 to 60	61 and over
	1	**2**	**3**	**4**	**6**	**8**
Heredity	No known history of heart disease	1 relative with cardiovascular disease over 60	2 relatives with cardiovascular disease over 60	1 relative with cardiovascular disease under 60	2 relatives with cardiovascular disease under 60	3 relatives with cardiovascular disease under 60
	1	**2**	**3**	**4**	**6**	**7**
Weight	More than 5 lbs. below standard weight	−5 to +5 lbs. standard weight	6–20 lbs. overweight	21–35 lbs. overweight	36–50 lbs. overweight	51–65 lbs. overweight
	0	**1**	**2**	**3**	**5**	**7**
Tobacco Smoking	Nonuser	Cigar and/or pipe	10 cigarettes or less a day	20 cigarettes a day	30 cigarettes a day	40 cigarettes a day or more
	0	**1**	**2**	**4**	**6**	**10**
Exercise	Intensive occupational and recreational exertion	Moderate occupational and recreational exertion	Sedentary work and intense recreational exertion	Sedentary occupational and moderate recreational exertion	Sedentary work and light recreational exertion	Complete lack of all exercise
	1	**2**	**3**	**5**	**6**	**8**
Cholesterol or Fat % in Diet	Cholesterol below 188 mg. Diet contains no animal or solid fat	Cholesterol 181–205 mg. Diet contains 10% animal or solid fats	Cholesterol 206–230 mg. Diet contains 20% animal or solid fats	Cholesterol 231–255 mg. Diet contains 30% animal or solid fats	Cholesterol 256–280 mg. Diet contains 40% animal or solid fats	Cholesterol 281–300 mg. Diet contains 50% animal or solid fats
	1	**2**	**3**	**4**	**5**	**7**
Blood Pressure	100 upper reading	120 upper reading	140 upper reading	160 upper reading	180 upper reading	200 or over reading
	1	**2**	**3**	**4**	**6**	**8**
Sex	Female under 40	Female 40–50	Female over 50	Male	Stocky male	Bald stocky
	1	**2**	**3**	**5**	**6**	**7**

Other risk factors – diabetes, stress and personality, electrocardiogram abnormalities, etc, are less directly measurable.
(−1 if taking regular and frequent exercise)
Average US diet contains 40% animal or solid fats.
Normal blood pressure reading is 120.

Adapted from 'Heart Risk' in *Go to Health*, New York: Dell Publishing

BE SAFE, NOT SORRY

Cigarettes and alcohol

Facts about smoking and the tobacco industry

- Smoking kills one in seven in the UK, and one in four regular smokers. It is the biggest single preventable cause of premature death.

- No other commonly available product is addictive in normal use and increases significantly the risk of death and disease.

- Governments have banned cigarette advertising for twenty years, but only from television. Of the teenagers surveyed in Northern Ireland, 75 per cent believed they had seen cigarette advertising on television.

- Tobacco companies sponsor over 300 hours of TV sport at a cost of around £10 million a year. Almost half of all seven to fifteen-year-olds watch the Embassy snooker final, where tobacco company coverage is equivalent to three 30 second slots an hour.

- Tobacco companies have bought product placements in the films *Superman II*, *Bond*, *Beverly Hills Cop* and *Roger Rabbit*.

- Most cigarette advertising takes the form of general, appealing images, rather than smoking.

- Most regular smokers start as children, often as young as ten to fourteen. Around 10 per cent of under-age teenagers smoke over fifty a week, a quarter of a million buy cigarettes, and nine out of ten of those they smoke they buy themselves.

- There has been little real change in the relative price of cigarettes in recent years.

- The tobacco industry is a major source of profits, exports and jobs in the UK. Tobacco sales yield £5 billion in tax revenue for the government.

ASSIGNMENTS ▷ ▷ ▷ ▷ ▷ ▷ ▷ ▷

1 Let members of your group take on roles as representatives of (a) the tobacco industry, (b) the government, (c) the medical profession, (d) the sports community, (e) young people, (f) smokers, (g) non-smokers, (h) a chair-person/presenter. Hold a discussion, prompted by questions from the rest of your group as a televised debate on the 'cost of smoking'.

2 Do you feel influenced by sports sponsorship on the part of tobacco companies? Write a memorandum as an executive in the tobacco industry recommending to your Board of Directors your proposal for sports sponsorship for the coming year. Be sure to explain the advantages to the company of your proposal.

3 To what extent do you feel that the facts above influence government policy towards smoking?

BE SAFE, NOT SORRY

Although most young people learn to drink moderately as they grow older, youthful drinking causes a variety of problems at home and at school. In one Scottish survey 2 per cent of girls and 3 per cent of boys reported losing a day's school through drinking; a third of seventeen-year-olds say drinking is a frequent cause of arguments with parents, causing more friction than smoking; only 20 per cent of teenage drinkers have not suffered any adverse consequences of drinking. Should there be health warnings on alcoholic drinks, as there are on packets of cigarettes? Or is there already a move afoot to discourage the nation from drinking?

CIGARETTES CAN SERIOUSLY DAMAGE YOUR HEALTH

CALIFORNIAN STATE LAW NOW REQUIRES ALL RETAILERS OF LIQUOR, INCLUDING WINE, TO DISPLAY A SIGN READING 'DRINKING MAY CAUSE BIRTH DEFECTS'.

WARNING: MORE THAN 30,000 PEOPLE DIE EACH YEAR IN THE UK FROM LUNG CANCER.
HM Government's Health Dept's Chief Medical Officers (warning on packets of cigarettes)

ALCOHOL . . .

ASSIGNMENTS ▷ ▷ ▷ ▷ ▷ ▷ ▷ ▷

1 Suggest a possible British health warning about alcohol.

2 Why are smoking, and drinking considered (a) a pleasure, and (b) bad for you?

3 What stops young people from (a) smoking and (b) drinking? Take a survey in the group to support your answer.

4 For most people drinking is enjoyable. Suggest ways of controlling your drinking.

BE SAFE, NOT SORRY

Drugs

What is the appeal of drugs to young people and what can be done to warn them of the dangers involved? Some youngsters are especially vulnerable and, as we see from the article opposite, good advice can even be counter-productive.

ASSIGNMENTS ▷ ▷ ▷ ▷ ▷ ▷ ▷ ▷

1 Why do you think the 'Heroin ad campaign' was unsuccessful in persuading young people of the risks of drugs?

2 Arrange your group to hold a court case, with lawyers representing the prosecution and defence and others called as witnesses in a judicial enquiry to investigate whether it should be made legal to produce, distribute and smoke cannabis.

3 In small groups, design your own advertising campaign to persuade young people not to take illegal drugs. This may use posters, radio or TV commercials as you see fit. Present your campaigns to the others in your Tutor Group and discuss the effectiveness of each.

BE SAFE, NOT SORRY

Heroin ad campaign is a flop

**by Brian Deer
Social Affairs
Correspondent**

THE government's high-profile campaign against heroin has failed to change key attitudes among young people at risk, according to a new research report. The finding contradicts claims by ministers that newspaper and television advertising is helping to tackle the crisis.

In January, David Mellor, the Home Office minister co-ordinating the drug effort, declared the £1.4m media campaign to have been a great success and Norman Fowler, the social services secretary, committed another £2m to advertising.

At the time, extracts from independent research were published which appeared to back up the claims. They showed that most young people had seen the advertising, were more likely to think heroin was a health risk and less inclined to say anything good about the drug.

But the full research findings show that attitudes hostile to heroin have been hardening only among those young people who are unlikely to come into contact with it. Among those most likely to have a choice about whether to take the drug, attitudes have moved in the wrong direction.

One of the most striking results is that young people who knew hard-drug users, and were therefore most at risk from future use, were less likely to say heroin was much more dangerous than cannabis after the campaign. In a two-stage survey, that figure fell from 52% to 42%.

'This is a very alarming shift in opinion,' said one market research analyst last week. 'This is terrible. The figure leaps out at me and says the campaign may have had precisely the opposite effect to the one the government wanted.'

Among males aged between 17 and 20, the number who thought heroin much more dangerous than cannabis fell from 54% to 46% and among all those aged between 19 and 20 the figure fell from 57% to 50%. The figure rose, however, among those who had no exposure to drugs and those who never smoked.

'These figures confirm our fears that the campaign had no effect on the problem,' said Leah Davidson, the coordinator of the City Roads crisis intervention centre in north London. 'Advertising may be good for vote-catching, but the money should be spent on projects that work.'

The research report, one of two 100-page studies of the campaign's effectiveness, also reveals a link between unemployment and heroin use, although that was also excluded from the government extracts published in January.

Ministers have consistently denied the connection. 'No link between the taking of drugs and unemployment has been established,' Mellor said last month in reply to Charles Kennedy, MP for Ross, Cromarty and Skye, and the Social Democratic spokesman on social services.

But the research, which was released last week, shows that most young people who had tried heroin were likely to be pro-smoking and drinking, bored, in conflict with parents, willing to take risks, anti-establishment, more often from low socio-economic groups and experiencing above-average unemployment. It confirms a recent study of drug misuse in Scotland which revealed that unemployed young people were between three and five times more likely to take drugs than those in full-time work.

From *The Sunday Times*, 9 March 1986

The conflicting ideals of life without stress

CHANGING TIMES
Lesley Garner

The unhappiest man in the idyllic Surrey village where I once lived was the gardener of the local manor. His gardens were an oasis of lush tranquillity. He had nothing to disturb him but the counterpoint of birdsong and the bass continuo of the bees. They carried him off eventually, victim of a nasty nervous breakdown brought on by the stress of his solitary job. Given all that time alone with the columbines and hollyhocks he had nothing to fill his brain but worry over the future of the human condition, mainly his.

Adam had much the same experience in the Garden of Eden. I think the forbidden tree was not the tree of knowledge at all but of stress. Even as Eve bit into the apple humankind was condemned to an eternity of worry.

In the United States, experts claim that three-quarters of America's workforce suffer from tension.

Overworked husbands find that the short time they grab at home in the evenings or weekends is consumed by rows. These high-speed relationships leave so little time for the gentle boring small-talk of married life, that the really important issues tend to pile up and get dealt with in a furious, often ineffective rush.

We are in danger of letting stress become the great 20th-century whinge. Without an element of stress, without the enlivening flow of adrenalin, without the quickening of brain that comes with a good idea or a successful sale or a skilfully manipulated meeting we would be vegetables. Anyone who has experienced the exhilaration of getting high on their work knows why it is worth staying late at the office.

The weary executive may apologise to his neglected wife and children, but if he were honest, he might admit that one of the many reasons he works a 14-hour day is because work is a more stimulating place than home.

You might think that a new generation of superwomen, who manage jobs and children might have a more realistic idea of what can be expected from family life than previous, more domesticated generations. But I wonder if they are not even more demanding. Women who have put in a hard day's work, who may suffer secret guilt over having their children cared for, and who earn as much money as their husbands, expect more from their partners, not less. If we can do it all, they think, how come the men still get away with doing one job and playing so little part at home?

This is the generation that insists on its men being in at the birth, on steering the Friday-night supermarket trolley, on cancelling the meeting in New York for the school carol concert and on sharing its feelings, too. It is the generation which has taken on the stresses of the male world, which wants its men to be New Men, sharing feminine tenderness and intuition. No wonder the stress factor between work and home is so great.

From the *Daily Telegraph*, 27 April 1988

ASSIGNMENTS ▷ ▷ ▷ ▷ ▷ ▷ ▷ ▷

1 Describe to a friend a time when you felt under stress.

2 Discuss with another pair what you could have done to cope with and even use the stress.

3 What do you learn about stress from the article from the *Daily Telegraph*?

4 How can you recognise harmful stress and 'enlivening' stress?

5 As a group, fill in a Table using the headings shown below.

6 Who can you consult if you need to seek help over stress?

Common reasons for stress	How stress affects your body and mind	How not to cope	How to cope

KNOW YOUR LAW

Civil and criminal law

There are two areas of law – civil and criminal. Laws to do with one individual's rights and obligations to another individual, such as trespassing on property or refusing to pay a debt or acting as a nuisance, are part of civil law. Individuals sue one another in the County Courts to enforce these rights and obligations, or to claim redress. Criminal law, on the other hand, is to do with claims against the individual by the whole of society for things like bad driving, or theft, or murder. These claims are brought by officers acting on behalf of society – the police, the Director of Public Prosecutions, and so on in Magistrates and Crown Courts.

ASSIGNMENTS ▷ ▷ ▷ ▷ ▷ ▷ ▷ ▷

1 When you buy something in a shop you have a contract: you pay money in exchange for goods of merchantable quality fit for their purpose. Explain why the shop's notice on the right is wrong (in fact it breaks the criminal law of the Fair Trading Act), and write a correct version.

2 When you trespass on someone's property he or she has an individual right to prevent you, by going to court if necessary. Explain why the farmer's notice is wrong and write a correct version.

NO REFUNDS ON
SALE GOODS
UNDER ANY
CIRCUMSTANCES

A notice in a clothes shop

TRESPASSERS WILL
BE PROSECUTED

A notice in a farmer's field

KNOW YOUR LAW

Civil law is concerned with matters such as tort, contract and family disputes. Tort is where one individual does wrong to another, such as trespass on property, trespass on the person, nuisance, negligence, slander or libel. Contracts are where one individual makes a legally binding agreement with another, for example to buy a house or to buy anything else or to work or provide a service of some kind. Here the issue is either about the existence of an agreement or the terms and performance of it. Family matters include the protection of children, and divorce and wills.

ASSIGNMENTS ▷ ▷ ▷ ▷ ▷ ▷ ▷ ▷

Set your room up as a courtroom, with three judges, two barristers for the plaintiffs (the injured party, first-named in each case) and two for the defendant. Let others act as witnesses if necessary and take turns, changing roles with each case. Notice that there is no jury in these civil cases. The lawyers should present the case for their clients, as summarised on the right. The judges then decide for plaintiff or defendant, and give their reasons, and award what they consider appropriate – perhaps contemptuous (for example, 1p) – damages.

1 Scott v. Shepherd
2 Donoghue v. Stevenson
3 Warner Brothers v. Nelson
4 Olley v. Marlborough Court Ltd

The answers are on the next page.

Four court cases

Scott v. Shepherd, (1773) 2 Wm. Bl. 892
On the evening of a fair-day at Milborne Port, Shepherd threw a lighted squib on to the market stall of one Yates who sold gingerbread. Then one Willis, in order to protect the wares of Yates, threw it away and it landed on the stall of one Ryal. He threw it to another part of the market house where it struck the plaintiff in the face, exploded and put out his eye.

Donoghue (or M'Alister) v. Stevenson, [1932] A.C 562
The appellant's friend purchased a bottle of ginger beer from a retailer in Paisley and gave it to her. The respondents were the manufacturers of the ginger beer. The appellant consumed some of the ginger beer and her friend was replenishing the glass, when, according to the appellant, the decomposed remains of a snail came out of the bottle. The bottle was made of dark glass so that the snail could not be seen until most of the contents had been consumed. The appellant became ill and served a writ on the manufacturers claiming damages.

Warner Brothers Pictures Incorporated v. Nelson, [1937] 1 K.B. 209
The defendant, the film actress Bette Davis, had entered into a contract in which she agreed to act exclusively for the plaintiffs for twelve months. She was anxious to obtain more money and so she left America, and entered into a contract with a person in England. The plaintiffs now asked for an injunction restraining the defendant from carrying out the English contract.

Olley v. Marlborough Court Ltd. [1949] 1 K.B. 532
Husband and wife arrived at an hotel as guests and paid for a room in advance. They went up to the room allotted to them; on one of the walls was the following notice: 'The proprietors will not hold themselves responsible for articles lost or stolen unless handed to the manageress for safe custody.' The wife closed the self-locking door of the bedroom and took the key downstairs to the reception desk. A third party took the key and stole certain of the wife's furs. In the ensuing action the defendants sought to rely on the notice as a term of contract.

KNOW YOUR LAW

The results of the court cases

Scott v. Shepherd

Held – Shepherd was liable for the injuries to Scott because there was no break in the chain of causation. Shepherd should have anticipated that Willis and Ryal would act as they did.

Donoghue (or M'Alister) v. Stevenson

The question before the House of Lords was whether the facts outlined above constituted a cause of action in negligence. The House of Lords *held* by a majority of three to two that they did. It was stated that a manufacturer of products, which are sold in such a form that they are likely to reach the ultimate consumer in the form in which they left the manufacturer with no possibility of intermediate examination, owes a duty to the consumer to take reasonable care to prevent injury. This rule has been broadened in subsequent cases so that the manufacturer is liable more often where defective chattels cause injury.

Warner Brothers Pictures Incorporated v. Nelson

Held – An injunction would be granted. The contract contained a negative stipulation not to work for anyone else, and this could be enforced. However, since the contract was an American one, the court limited the operation of the injunction to the area of the court's jurisdiction, and although the contract stipulated that the defendant would not work in any other occupation, the injunction was confined to work on stage or screen.

Olley v. Marlborough Court Ltd

Held – The contract was completed at the reception desk and no subsequent notice could effect the plaintiff's rights.

 N.B. As was pointed out in *Spurling v. Bradshaw*, [1956] 1 W.L.R. 461, if the husband and wife had seen the notice on a previous visit to the hotel it would have been binding on them.

KNOW YOUR LAW

The police and young people

Answer true or false to each of the following statements (answers on page 159).

The police have a right to:
1 stop you in the street and ask you questions.
2 search you, your bag or vehicle without a warrant.
3 hold you at the police station without informing anyone for twenty-four hours.
4 your signed statement, if they arrest you.
5 hold you for up to twenty-four hours before charging you with an offence.

You have a right to:
6 refuse to answer questions.
7 swear or shout at the police if they persist in asking you questions that you have refused to answer.
8 refuse to go with the police if asked to help them with their enquiries.
9 have access to a solicitor for free, and at any time of the day or night, if arrested.
10 refuse to have your fingerprints and photograph taken.

ASSIGNMENTS ▷ ▷ ▷ ▷ ▷ ▷ ▷ ▷

1 Compare your answers to the questions above with the answers on page 159 and the results of the others in your group.

2 Do you think that the police have too little or too much power to investigate the actions and intentions of private individuals? Which should take priority – the rights of the individual or the needs of society as a whole?

3 Discuss your view of the police with the others in your group. How often have you spoken with the police, in what context and what were your feelings at the time? How and why do you think attitudes to the police differ between your generation and that of your parents/guardians?

4 Crimes must generally involve both a criminal act and a criminal intention, and must be proven in court beyond a reasonable doubt. How do you think these requirements affect the work of the police?

USING YOUR VOTE

When you become eighteen your name is placed on the electoral role for the area where you live and you become part of the country's electorate. Suddenly you have a vote that is worth just as much as your tutor's, your parent/guardian's, or the prime minister's, and you can vote in whatever way you wish in local government and parliamentary elections. Will you use your vote? Will you use it wisely?

Most people take the responsibility of voting very seriously. They see this not just as a duty where they share in running the country but also as their chance to express their feelings within the democratic system, and to stand side by side with every other citizen of the country on an equal basis. But responsibility can make people become anxious, as anyone who has been inside a polling station, or even worked as a polling officer will know.

Mr Ellis versus the people

Mr Ellis, Mr Martin and Petula are working away non-stop at the polling station.
From outside we hear a voice calling through the loudspeaker of a car.

LOUDSP 1   Today is polling day. Today is polling day. Vote for the party that cares. Vote Labour.

Another voice on a loudspeaker is heard from another car.

LOUDSP 2   Today is polling day. Vote Liberal – the party that –
LOUDSP 1   Vote Labour. Today is polling day –
LOUDSP 2   Change to Liberal. Vote Liberal today –
MR E   (*to Petula*) Get the constable to clear Simon and Garfunkel away, will you? They know they're not allowed near here.

She gets up and goes.

MR W   You know what I've done, don't you? Brought my laundry list, and left my polling card on the mantelpiece . . .
MR M   That's alright, if I can just have your . . .
MR W   No, hang on! (*He searches through his wallet*) I've left them *both* on the mantelpiece . . . Gordon Walmsley, 18 Wellington Street.

Mr Martin searches his register, ticks off the name, Mr Ellis stamps the next ballot paper, and gives it to Mr Martin who hands it to Mr Walmsley.

MR M   Thank you.
MR W   You're welcome.

He starts to exit.

MR M   Aren't you going to vote?
MR W   (*turning*) Eh? (*Realises what he's doing*) Oh, yes. (*He turns back and goes to a booth to vote*)

USING YOUR VOTE

Cut to a voter – Mr Crabtree – in one of the booths. He turns and calls to them.

MR C   Excuse me! Are you there?

MR E   Hello?

MR C   I've voted for the wrong one.

MR E   Sorry?

MR C   I've put it in the wrong square.

MR E   Bring me the ballot paper, sir. I'll give you another.

Mr Crabtree goes to the desk and gives Mr Ellis his spoiled paper.

MR C   It's only nerves.

MR E   Easily done.

MR C   Like taking your exams in a way, isn't it?

MR E   Well . . . not really.

Mrs Mobberley, in her 60s, approaches the desk.

MRS M   Conservative.

MR M   What??

MRS M   Conservative, please. Thank you.

She starts to go out again.

MR E   A moment, madam, please. (*She stops*) Do you have your polling card?

MRS M   My who?

MR E   It should have come in the post.

MRS M   I've never had one. There's all sorts of stuff I never get.

MR E   No . . . well, can you tell me your name and address, please?

MRS M   I've had a leaflet about learning Kung-Fu.

MR M   Can I have your name and address, please.

MRS M   I thought it was supposed to be secret?

MR M   Not your name and address. Only your *vote*.

MRS M   Conservative.

MR M   (*agitated*) You mustn't tell us. That's the whole object of the ballot! We have to give you a ballot-paper, then you go across there and . . .

MRS M   Just because you lot's nowt better to do, it doesn't mean to say *I* haven't . . . Sat here polishing your breeches behinds all day . . . You drive us silly to come and vote and then when we do . . . (*She simmers down, and snaps her name out*) Mrs Mobberley, 47 Charlotte Street.

MR M   (*relieved*) Thank you, madam.

MRS M   Conservative.

Mr Martin stares after her, the morning's frustrations and exasperations boiling up. They finally explode.

USING YOUR VOTE

MR M   We're supposed to be the most politically sophisticated society in the world! Alastair Burnet's always saying so! Robert Mackenzie nearly wets himself saying so! All they've to do is identify themselves, make a bloody cross on a piece of bloody paper, stick it in a bloody box and go home! And they can't! Every single one of them's a bloody . . .

From J. Rosenthal 'Mr Ellis Versus The People' in *P'tang, Yang, Kipperbang*, Longman Imprint, 1984

ASSIGNMENTS ▷ ▷ ▷ ▷ ▷ ▷ ▷ ▷

1 Find three references that emphasise the importance of people making up their own minds about how to vote without unfair influence from others.

2 Who in your household has the vote? How seriously do they use it? Do they vote in every election and do they make up their minds which way to vote carefully or not?

3 Mr M: 'I'm not going to vote myself – I can't see the point.' Write a scene to continue the play, starting with this line, and including a discussion (either serious or humorous) between the characters in the extract above.

General Election – majority party in each region

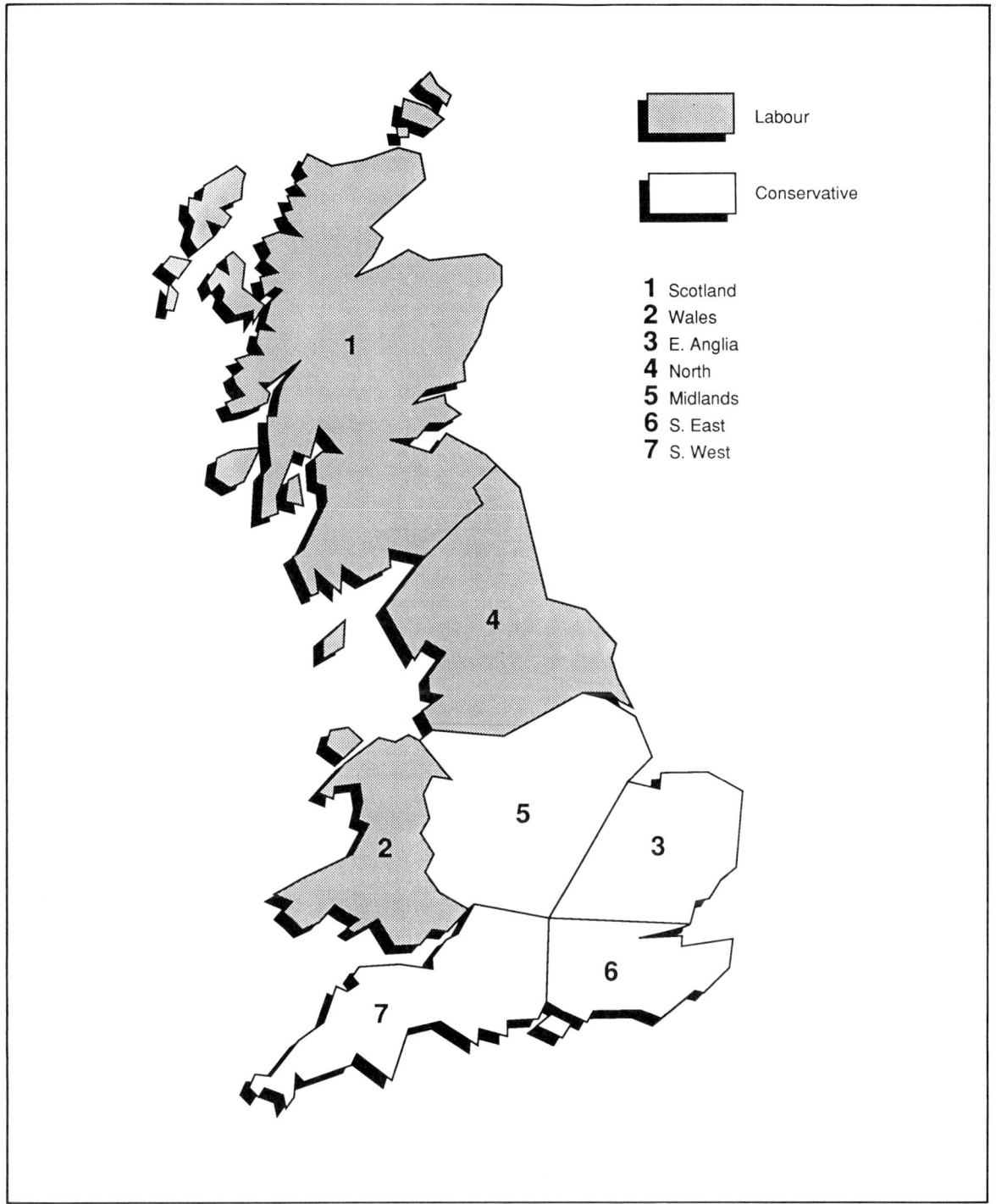

Labour

Conservative

1 Scotland
2 Wales
3 E. Anglia
4 North
5 Midlands
6 S. East
7 S. West

USING YOUR VOTE

General Election – result in Greater London

Based on a map in I. Crewe and A. Fox, *British Parliamentary Constituencies – A Statistical Compendium*, Faber and Faber, 1984

ASSIGNMENTS ▷ ▷ ▷ ▷ ▷ ▷ ▷ ▷

1 Summarise the distribution of seats by political parties as shown on page 117 for the 1983 General Election. Why do you think the country voted in this way? Do you see these broad voting patterns as evidence that the country is divided or not?

2 Find out the names of the ward, local authority(ies), local councillors, constituency and Member of Parliament for wherever you live. Find out the main political proposals of the parties represented at the most recent election in your area. Let a few of your group act as politicians standing on different party tickets and conduct pre-election meetings followed by a secret ballot of the Tutor Group.

3 Explain how it is that, even if equal numbers of votes were cast nationally for the Labour, Conservative and SLD parties, the allocation of seats could still be as shown opposite. Do you think that this 'first past the post' electoral system is the best one? Research in your local library as necessary, then devise an alternative system that you prefer.

USING YOUR VOTE

Sex and politics

Why are there so few Linda Chalkers, Renee Shorts, Margaret Thatchers in politics? Is it because in general women lack the motivation, the deep, overriding hunger for success and power, the driving, self-centred will to achieve that seemingly motivate so many of their male contemporaries? Or is it a case of men possessing the sort of traits which facilitate success in the rough-and-tumble of the political arena, whereas so-called feminine traits, which may be all very well for child-rearing and housekeeping, are just not what the Speaker orders?

Politics certainly emphasises competition, assertiveness, aggression even, and there are studies of children at play which suggest that from an early age boys manifest ways of behaving which will stand them in good stead if they should, in adult life, decide to seek a career influencing other people.

On average, boys play competitively whereas girls play cooperatively. But there is the important qualification that in general, boys and girls do not differ all that much. The differences are, in the main, due to a relatively small but significant number who lead their sex in a combative style (boys) or collaborative fashion (girls).

In one experiment which involved a number of boys and girls having to persuade their peers to eat some bitter-tasting chocolate biscuits, the boys employed a mixture of bullying coercion and blatant lies, whereas the girls promised a share of the reward or personal friendship. In a political world where the levers of power are pulled by a mixture of physical dominance and verbal deceits, men would seem to have the gifts required.

But perhaps it is merely a question of a lack of ambition on the part of the great mass of women.

After all, when a woman such as Mrs Thatcher or Barbara Castle wants to climb the ladder of power, she does. Research study after study can find no fault with female intelligence, academic ability or motivation. Women do as well as men at school and at university. Men and women undertaking similar jobs report equivalent attitudes to work, commitment and job satisfaction. What is of interest, however, concerns the degree of self-confidence shown by the two sexes.

Men are consistently more self-confident than women and are more inclined to take the credit for their own success. In contrast, women are more likely to attribute success to luck or external circumstances.

Even when men and women perform at comparable levels of competence, they differ in their self-assessment. For example, immediately following an examination, women tend to emerge feeling they have done badly, men feeling they have done well, despite examination results indicating no difference in actual performance between the sexes.

Is it, then, a question of fear of failure and an actual avoidance of success that accounts for the relative lack of women at the top? After all, it cannot simply be a matter of numbers, for even in those jobs and professions where women are numerically strong, such as teaching and social work, they are less well represented at key administrative levels and in senior positions.

Some women do excuse their reluctance to take more responsibility by expressing the wish to retain contact with the grass roots, the 'shop floor' or the clinical situation. But possibly a more important factor is the extent to which married women working full-time are still expected to undertake a disproportionate amount of the cleaning, cooking, washing and servicing of the household compared with their full-time husbands.

It is not merely the practical aspects of home care that are seen to be particularly 'feminine' tasks. The emotional aspects of child care are more likely to be the working woman's responsibilities than the working man's. Over and over again, in countries as seemingly progressive and egalitarian as Sweden, the Netherlands and the Soviet Union, full-time working women end up putting substantial hours into looking after the home, the children, even the au pair, domestic help or nanny if there is one.

Given such a disparity between the sexes, it is almost certainly asking too much of women to give the 100% commitment which many employers, professions and occupations implicitly demand of their workers. It is hardly surprising, therefore, that many women who do enter and succeed in politics are, to a very large extent, 'supermen', tough, ambitious, assertive *and* capable of two jobs instead of one.

In practice, however, the majority of women in politics are not representative of women in general, and a disproportionate number of women in politics are single, widowed or divorced, have had their children reared or are married to extremely wealthy men.

Of course individual women will succeed and doubtless there will be some shift. But the Houses of Parliament, with their remarkable hours, their bars, their customs imbued with the traditions of the public school and the university union, seem likely to remain the male bastions they are for many years to come.

From Anthony W. Clare in *The Sunday Times*, 23 March 1986

USING YOUR VOTE

ASSIGNMENTS ▷ ▷ ▷ ▷ ▷ ▷ ▷ ▷

1 Would you like to stand as a political candidate in an election one day? Do you think you would make a good politician? Name one other person in your Tutor Group who you think might do the job better than you, and say why.

2 Pick out those in your group who received most nominations in assignment 1. The rest of the group, acting as their local political party who wish to appoint a young people's candidate for a forthcoming election, should interview them, if they agree.

3 How much respect do you have for leading, national politicians? What can be done to ensure that there are enough women in such positions of authority? Does the country get the politicians it deserves?

DECISIONS

A general approach

How good are you at making up your mind? Do you find it easier to decide between major choices such as subject options than minor choices such as what TV programme to watch? Do you ever regret having made the wrong decision about your personal life?

We must all take decisions. We choose what to do and how to do it from the moment we get up in the morning, or do not, to when we go to sleep at night, or do not! Most decisions we take for granted, many are based on habits, and many more are taken for us as we follow what others do or what they tell us to do. But many jobs are all to do with taking decisions. Jobs, careers and other opportunities depend on how we decide what we want to do, can do, or should do. How can we help to steer ourselves so that we make the right decisions in the best possible way?

- Start with a clear aim.
- Then find out all you need to know. What tools do you have? What help? How much time? What are the advantages and disadvantages?

Finally make your choice between clear alternatives. Do you want to do this course or that, or go to this college or that, or work at this job or that one?

Your own decisions about your work are very important to you but as you become more and more involved in them, it can become more difficult to choose wisely. Nevertheless you should try, so set out your aims, find out all you need to know, the advantages and disadvantages, then consider between alternatives.

Survival at sea

Steven Callahan was shipwrecked, afloat for seventy-six days with no food or water in a tiny liferaft. Yet he survived.

ASSIGNMENTS ▷ ▷ ▷ ▷ ▷ ▷ ▷ ▷

1 Imagine that you were in Callahan's situation. Decide your aims. Make a list on your own first. Then compare your aims with those of the others in your group. Now try to agree on an order of priorities. Is it easier to make decisions on your own or as a group? Which is the way to take the *best* decisions.

2 Find from the diagram how he decided to solve each problem and what equipment he used to help him.

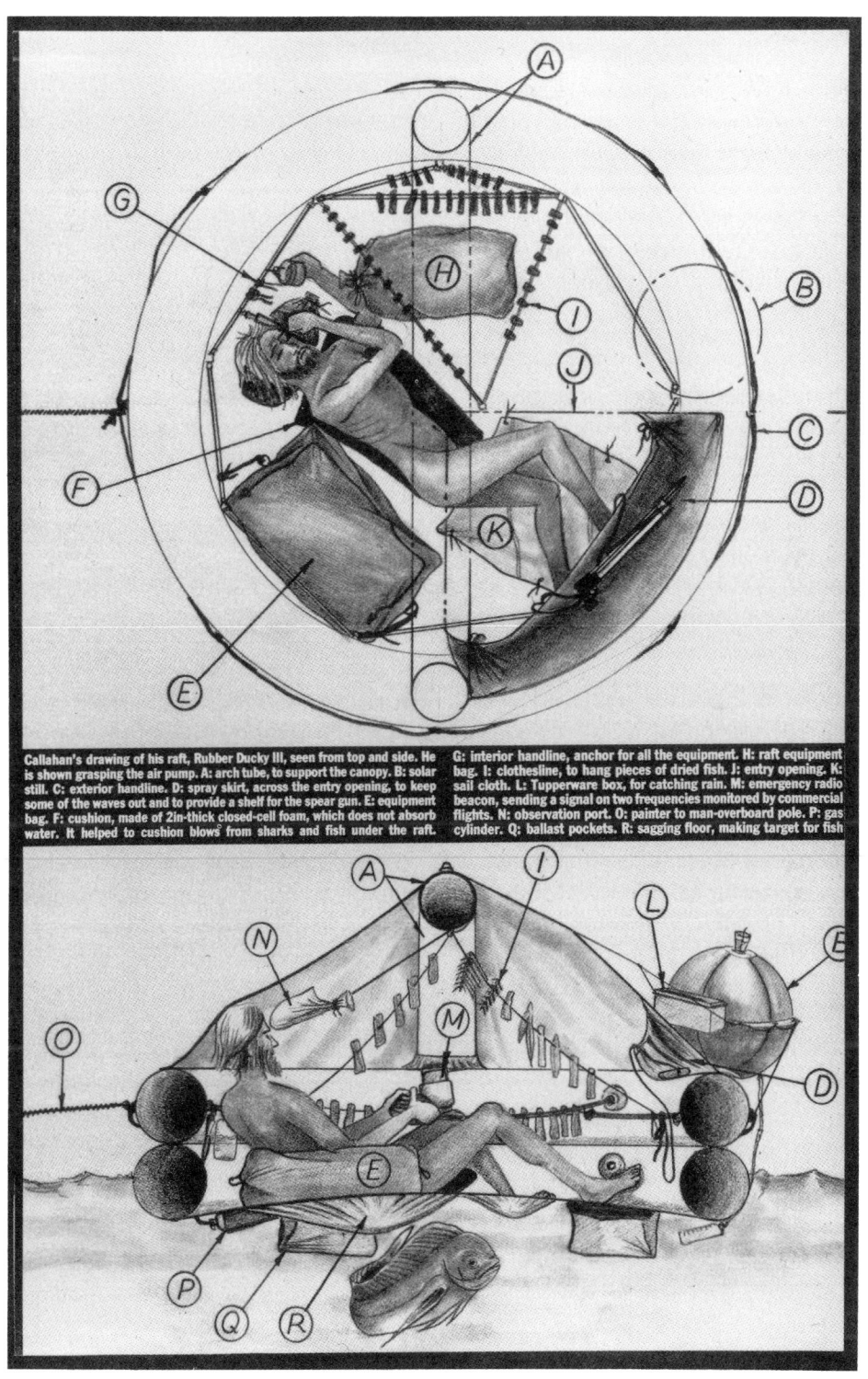

Callahan's drawing of his raft, Rubber Ducky III, seen from top and side. He is shown grasping the air pump. A: arch tube, to support the canopy. B: solar still. C: exterior handline. D: spray skirt, across the entry opening, to keep some of the waves out and to provide a shelf for the spear gun. E: equipment bag. F: cushion, made of 2in-thick closed-cell foam, which does not absorb water. It helped to cushion blows from sharks and fish under the raft. G: interior handline, anchor for all the equipment. H: raft equipment bag. I: clothesline, to hang pieces of dried fish. J: entry opening. K: sail cloth. L: Tupperware box, for catching rain. M: emergency radio beacon, sending a signal on two frequencies monitored by commercial flights. N: observation port. O: painter to man-overboard pole. P: gas cylinder. Q: ballast pockets. R: sagging floor, making target for fish

DECISIONS

'The Prisoner's Dilemma'

Most decisions have something to do with other people. Your own decision may affect them in some way, or you may make a shared decision where you must work with other people. But is it better to work for yourself to try to outwit other people, or to work with others so that you all gain together? Do the 'nice guys' finish first or last?

Put yourself in a position where you must make this simple choice – to work with people or against them in a game called 'The Prisoner's Dilemma'. Set yourself a simple aim – to get as much as possible out of the game by scoring between one and four points each go. Then choose a 'partner' to play the game with/against, as follows.

Each player makes a decision either to 'co-operate' with the other, or to 'defect'. They decide at the same time (no rush) and in secret. But they make their decisions with the knowledge that their score depends on what they *both* decide. If both co-operate they score three each; if both defect they score two each. If one co-operates and the other defects, however, the co-operator scores only one while the defector scores four. When both players are ready they show their decisions on paper at the same time.

Start by playing the game once only, with every other person in the group. Then play again, but play for twenty goes against just one partner, preferably one whom you do not know well. Play first, then read on.

What do you find? When this game is played it often turns out the same way. In once-off decisions 'defecting' is always the dominant strategy. Nice guys who co-operate with their fellows seem to do worst. But in continued runs it is possible to establish more successful strategies. The best is apparently to start 'nicely' – by co-operating. If both co-operate they gain the best scores overall. But if one partner defects, the best response is a 'tit for tat' swift 'retaliation' in the following go. This shows that defecting does not pay. Quick forgiveness in the go after that sets the pattern for mutual success once more. By starting 'nice', offering swift retaliation and forgiveness and playing a long-term game together, both partners gain most. Is there a lesson there for us all?

Do you prefer working for yourself or with other people? Do you enjoy a challenge with the chance to really get on if you succeed, or do you prefer to take things at your own pace so that you feel secure? Do you like having a place of your own or getting out and about? These are the sorts of opportunities that are offered to you in work but it is a very special sort of job that offers you everything you would like. Often it is better to start by thinking about what you yourself can offer rather than what you can get out of it. Do you have the necessary qualities in order to get on with the people there? Can you make good use of the resources that will be put your way?

Below is a story about a shopkeeper in a remote Himalayan village.

The Village Shopkeeper

The shopkeeper's prices were higher than they should have been. The villagers could do nothing about it.

They had nowhere else to go. But, unknown to him, a bright teenager was planning to challenge his monopoly and to bring down the cost of essentials.

The boy always hung around the shop lending the owner a helping hand, carrying heavy loads, running errands – and watching his uncle, the shopkeeper, and learning.

He would open a shop to compete with his uncle and would lower the prices. The village would benefit – and so would he, for he knew that he could easily make a profit without overcharging. But one cannot start a shop with no capital.

He still had no savings, but the buffalo he had acquired produced milk, and milk could be sold. But not in the village. Shanti bought a second buffalo with borrowed money and drove the two beasts to a more prosperous area where milk commanded a good price.

Life in the hills was hard enough, but this was proving harder. He rose at 3 o'clock in the morning to milk the cattle and walked through the jungle to the road to catch the bus into town. At first he sold the milk wherever he could, gradually winning a name for himself as one of the few milkmen who didn't add water to it. He acquired a dozen regular customers dispersed all over the town, but didn't grudge the hours of walking: regular customers produced an assured income.

Other milkmen were content to make one delivery a day. Not Shanti. He returned from town, exhausted, to collect leaves and grass in the jungle, took the buffaloes to the stream, some distance from his shack, and then he milked them for his second delivery. He made a clear profit of roughly 300 rupees (about £16) a month. Most of this went on food for the family, but some he managed to save.

Shanti made occasional trips to the village, ostensibly to work in his fields. But he always carried a few packets of tea, boxes of matches, lentils, and sold them to his neighbours at prices lower than in the village shop. Sometimes they asked him to bring to the village things that could be obtained more cheaply in town. It was too insignificant a fraction of the village shop's turnover to worry his uncle.

He had not managed to accumulate all the capital he needed, but he returned to the village, for good, with a larger selection of merchandise than he had ever brought before. Yet it was as nothing compared with the shopkeeper's stock.

Shanti's one-room dwelling became a shop during the day and the family's sleeping quarters at night. His prices were 10 to 20 per cent lower than in the village shop. 'I give him six months,' his uncle, the shopkeeper, said. He knew something Shanti didn't.

Shanti's customers were no longer paying cash. They now patronised his shop only if he let them have credit. In order to be able to extend it, he was compelled to go into debt himself. More customers came, his turnover grew little by little, and his profits increased in step with it. But he continued to keep his prices lower and to work much harder than the old shopkeeper.

His business increased, but he had to borrow more and more to keep it going – to finance, in effect, his debtors. When he implored them to pay up, they usually said they just did not have the money, and it was true.

The old man had always known something about his challenger that Shanti did not know himself: he did not have the ruthlessness required of a village shopkeeper.

The villagers' sympathies were still with him, but that would not do him much good.

He was on the verge of bankruptcy.

From Victor Zorza, 'Village Voice' in *The Times*, 2 June 1986

ASSIGNMENTS ▷ ▷ ▷ ▷ ▷ ▷ ▷ ▷

1 Why did Shanti want to be a shopkeeper? Explain whether you could see yourself doing the same thing, or not.

2 What qualities do you think Shanti had that would help him to be a good shopkeeper? What might he have lacked?

3 What resources, beside his own time and effort, did Shanti need to become a shopkeeper? In what ways would it be easier, or harder, for you to set up shop locally compared with the Himalayan village where Shanti lived?

OPPORTUNITIES IN WORK

Working with other people

Let's say that you are setting out to find work, paid or voluntary, and that you have a choice. You look at what different jobs can offer you, and what you have to offer in return. You may be tempted to see your opportunities in terms of the tasks you will be asked to perform or the money you will earn, or the clothes you will wear. But do not forget that in almost all jobs you will work with **people**.

You may be providing a service to others, either as a volunteer or as a paid worker. Indirectly, your teachers are serving you, the students, in this way. You may be part of a team – as your teachers are members of staff working together to run the school or college. And whatever your own position in the team – as leader or follower, thinker or doer – you have the opportunity to work together with other people.

ASSIGNMENTS ▷ ▷ ▷ ▷ ▷ ▷ ▷ ▷

1 Look at page 128. Suppose that you are Head of Personnel in a business. What 'personal qualities' would you look for in appointing someone:
   • to join the Research and Development Department?
   • to join the external relations side of the Distribution Department?
   • as Chief Financial Manager?

2 Take on different roles in your group as managers in charge of each of the departments shown in the example on page 128 under the leadership of the General Manager. Invite the remaining members of the group to come for interviews with the management team for work as school leavers joining the business. Make sure you cover the following areas in each interview:
   • the opportunities offered in work for your business;
   • the skills and qualities offered by each job applicant;
   • the most suitable area of work within the business for each applicant.

You might like to refer to page 154 before starting.

People and Business

It is easy to think of business as a mass of offices, factories, money and products. In fact, business is really the combined efforts of working people.

Business creates a great variety of jobs and they are suited to people with differing personal qualities; the creative, the logical, the ambitious, the caring and the methodical. Different skills and different qualities are needed within every enterprise.

Take a look at the different functions which make up a business:-

A Research and Development
Scientists, engineers, and designers, all striving to create new services and products.

B Marketing . . . Identifies the need for new services and products, and finds the best way of supplying the need. It studies the reaction to new services and products, and finds out how much the customers are prepared to pay.

C Distribution . . . People to deal direct with customers, wholesalers and retailers. People to work out the most efficient transport methods, since the product may have to go all over the world.

D Personnel . . . People who deal with recruitment, training, salaries, pensions, health, welfare, safety and often industrial relations as well.

E Financial Management . . . Management accountants work closely with all the other managers and supply information to help them control the business and make decisions about the future.

F General Management . . . Make decisions about a company's future on the basis of information and advice provided by a range of specialist managers including the management accountant.

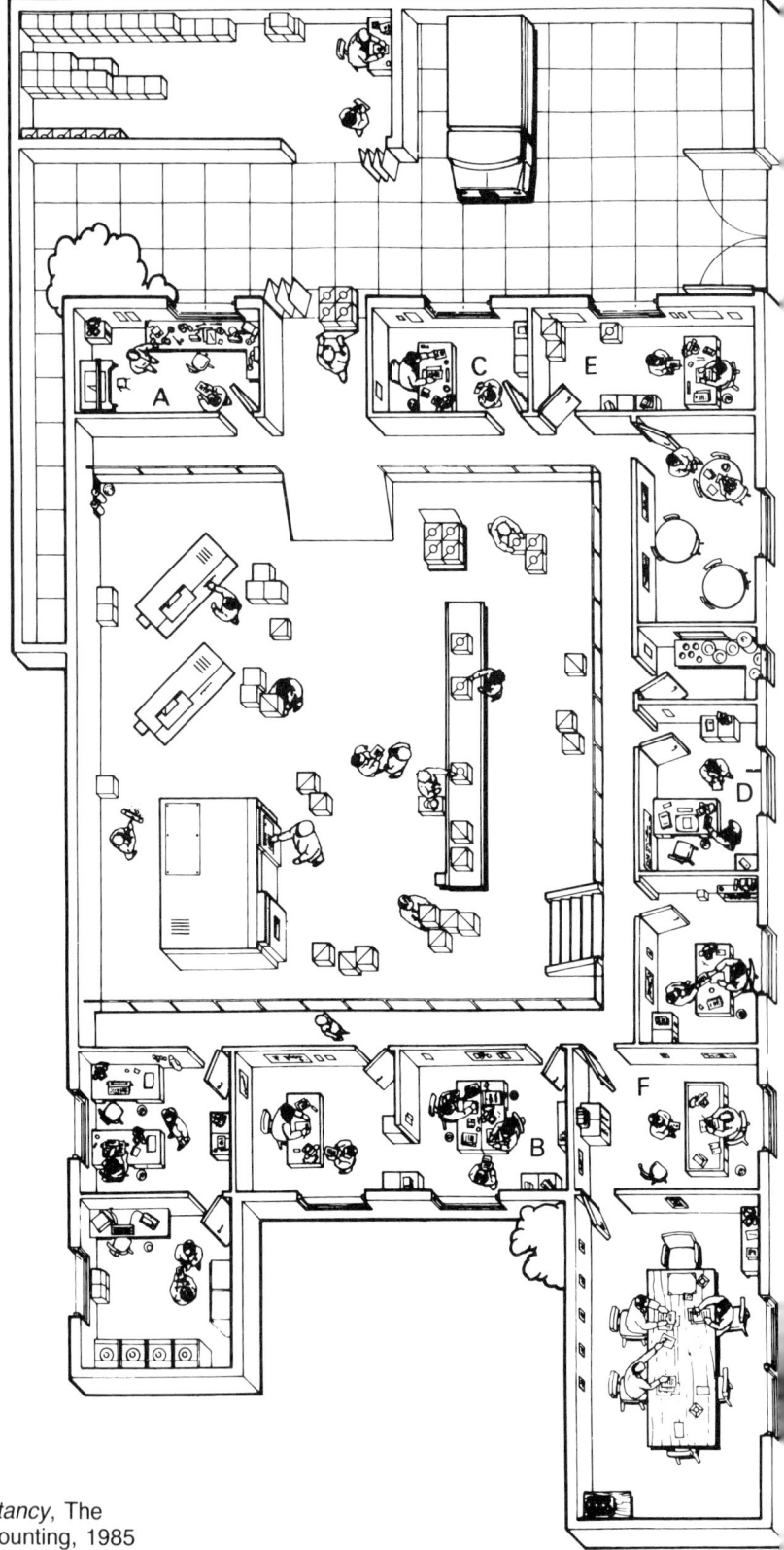

From *Careers in Management Accountancy*, The Institute of Cost and Management Accounting, 1985

MEET THE WELFARE STATE

When are you entitled to benefits?

How good are you at looking after yourself? Could you earn a living for yourself if you had to? Could you keep yourself in accommodation, food, drink and clothes? While you are young, fit and healthy it may not be a problem to provide for yourself in these ways, but what if something goes wrong? For that you need some sort of insurance, but even insurance costs money. The welfare state aims to provide basic insurance (called social security) to every person in the country 'from the cradle to the grave'.

You pay in to the scheme when you are earning money and according to how much you earn. Then people who cannot get work, or are ill, or disabled, or retired, are paid benefits of different kinds with your money. But what entitles people to receive benefits, and is the system fair?

The social security system

Contributions paid in

* 'National Insurance – employees' contributions rise as a proportion of income, up to a fixed limit. Employers contribute as well

Benefits paid out

* Unemployment benefit if available for work and enough contributions have been paid

* Housing benefit to cover basic living accommodation

* Supplementary benefit to get enough money to live on

* Child benefit to the mother of dependent children

* Benefits to the disabled, those kept off work by sickness or injury, those entitled to free dental or medical care, or other special cases

* State pensions for the elderly, paid for from current contributions by those in work

ASSIGNMENTS ▷ ▷ ▷ ▷ ▷ ▷ ▷ ▷

In groups of three or four discuss each of these propositions and try to agree either for or against, with reasons that you can present to the rest of your Tutor Group.

- People should be allowed to opt out of the welfare state.
- People should pay equal shares of their earnings as national insurance contributions.
- Both employers and employees should continue to pay contributions.
- People should not be able to get both supplementary and unemployment benefit.
- Benefits are closely related to need.
- The benefits system is so complicated that it puts people off claiming what they are entitled to.
- Child benefits encourage people to have too many children.
- It is better to pay benefits as money that people can spend for themselves rather than as personal services such as health care, education, accommodation, or meals on wheels.

Hippies 'a band of brigands'

THE 300-strong hippy 'peace convoy', branded by Mr Hurd, Home Secretary, yesterday as 'a band of mediaeval brigands', huddled miserably together in the New Forest rain last night as Forestry Commission lawyers in London issued an application for a legal possession order that will lead to the hippies' eviction.

The convoy, weary, fed-up and running low on cash and supplies, sensed that Stoney Cross Plain, to which they drove on Sunday night, may see the end of their dream of a grand gathering to celebrate the June 21 summer solstice at Stonehenge. They have offended too many sensitivities in the West Country and society's response is imminent, it seems.

The authorities had virtually put the group in quarantine, well away from the society they say they reject in favour of an 'alternative' culture and with few of the conveniences on which they nevertheless rely.

Local Department of Employment and DHSS benefit offices in the area now aware that the group is likely to be around for a few days, yesterday made emergency staffing arrangements for the weekly pay-out of State benefits. With 300 people about to receive over £35 each, more than £10,000 in cash or Giro cheques could be involved.

The relatively few married couples among the hippies will get about £47 between them in either unemployment benefit or supplementary benefit and those with children will get an extra £10 for each child. The DHSS benefit office at Totton, near Southampton, the nearest to the hippy camp, normally pays out to 50 callers a week.

DHSS officials admitted last night that their staff travel with the hippy convoy wherever they go – to make sure they get all their handouts. The Department is understood to have launched the scheme last year and the taxpayer has been footing the bill ever since.

From the *Daily Telegraph*, 4 June 1986

ASSIGNMENTS ▷ ▷ ▷ ▷ ▷ ▷ ▷ ▷

1 Write a letter to a newspaper **either** as a hippy justifying your lifestyle and right to state benefits, or as a retired local resident complaining about 'scrounging hippies'.

2 Choose two of your group to act as social security officers and the rest to act as a group of hippies. Imagine that the hippies have come to the local office of social security and that the officers must:

(a) find out the relevant circumstances;

(b) explain to the hippies what benefits they may be entitled to;

(c) decide what benefits to pay to each individual.

JOBS, CAREERS AND YOU

Choosing jobs and careers

There was a time when you could expect to take on a job for the whole of your working life – as a blacksmith or writer or district nurse perhaps. But for most of us those days have gone. Now you can expect to change your line of work three times or so on average, and to retrain and move home as you do so. In 1981, for example, there were job changes affecting on average one in three of the workforce.

How should you set about choosing jobs and careers, now or in the future? Most people probably wait until the right offer comes along and with one in eight of the workforce unemployed there are many who must take the first job they can find. But most job changes are to similar sorts of work, so it is best to choose the right line carefully. Try to find out what will suit you personally; as well as what different jobs have to offer.

What to look for in yourself

What will you look for in a job? Do you want to make lots of money or do you want to do something that you feel worthwhile in its own right? Do you want the chance to meet people and help them, or to face new challenges and have the opportunity for promotion? Are there other considerations that matter more to you than these? If you ask yourself the right questions, there is a chance that you will work out some answers, some decisions, in your own mind. But it may well be the case that you will learn more about yourself if you talk to other people and answer their questions instead. Remember that you must look not only at what you feel like now, but also at what will matter to you in ten, twenty or forty years time.

Next, look at what you have to offer in terms of abilities and character; and the jobs to which you may be best suited. What are your interests, abilities and personality? The following guide may help you, again, to ask the right questions so that you can see what sort of work to look for. Perhaps you could look for a career that is creative and persuasive, such as journalism; or helpful and physical, such as nursing; or organising and persuasive, such as marketing and sales work.

JOBS, CAREERS AND YOU

What type of work will I find most interesting?

Interests

- Make a list of everything you have enjoyed doing at school.
- Now add everything you enjoyed doing in any jobs you have had.
- Finally add to your list all the things you have enjoyed doing in your leisure time.

Opposite, we have printed a number of different groups of interests – pick out the two (or at most three) categories which correspond most closely to your list of what you have enjoyed doing at school or in leisure time.

Abilities

Make a new list of what you have been good at:

- in your school studies
- in any jobs you have done
- in what you have done at home or in your leisure activities outside school.

For your school subjects ask yourself exactly what you were good at doing; for example in the sciences were you good at understanding and applying the principles, or good at doing experiments? If you were good at languages were you better on the grammar side, or on the literature side interpreting and explaining the meaning and importance of different characters or styles?

Again in your leisure activities, ask yourself exactly what you were good at, for example using your hands or working out the best way to get things done.

In the same way as you worked out *interests*, identify which two (or three) of the categories opposite best describe the ways in which you have been good at doing things at school, in jobs or at home and in your leisure activities.

Personality

Now think about what has happened:

- at school
- in jobs
- at home and in your leisure activities.

When have you had problems to overcome? When have you been worried, anxious or depressed?

From these situations you should be able to pick out two (or at most three) categories which describe your strongest qualities – the qualities which have enabled you to put up with and cope with different problems and difficulties.

JOBS, CAREERS AND YOU

Career types

Type	Interests	Abilities	Personality
CREATE	Artistic	Inventive	Imaginative
HELP	Assisting	Fluent	Sociable
INVESTIGATE	Researching	Analytical	Flexible
ORGANISE	Co-ordinating	Methodical	Reliable
PERSUADE	Influencing	Leading	Determined
PHYSICAL	Active	Energetic	Resilient
PRACTICAL	Producing	Manual	Thorough

From the Association of Graduate Careers Advisory Services,
What do Graduates do? 1985, Hobsons Ltd, 1984

ASSIGNMENTS ▷ ▷ ▷ ▷ ▷ ▷ ▷ ▷

1 Make up your own lists of interests, abilities and situations that show qualities and personality as suggested.

2 Consider the list of 'career types' shown. Think about all of the others in your Tutor Group and write down the two career types that seem, to you, to be likely to suit each of them best. Then take it in turns in your group to compare suggestions. How does each individual's own self-assessment compare with that of the group?

JOBS, CAREERS AND YOU

What to look for in a job

It is difficult to choose between options when you know little or nothing about them. So how can you find out what different jobs involve? Certainly you can read the guide books and pamphlets in the careers room, or you can order them from professional bodies such as the Law Society. You can ask your teachers, tutors or careers staff for their ideas. But no tips are better than those 'straight from the horse's mouth' so it is well worth talking to people who do the work that you are interested in. It would be better still take a short introductory course, or go work-shadowing or apply for holiday work. In fact, any first-hand experience in the area that interests you will be helpful. Try to decide a 'shortlist' of a few jobs that appeal to you and then find out about them. This way you can choose on the basis of what you do know about each job and so avoid a serious mistake.

English

Examples of the destinations of 193 students who graduated from three universities and one college of higher education in 1988.

FURTHER FULL-TIME STUDY: 56 graduates

14 higher degree
20 Postgraduate Certificate in Education
5 Diploma in Journalism
3 Teaching English as a Foreign Language preparatory certificate
3 Diploma in Computing
2 drama course
2 Diploma in Publishing
1 Bar exam
1 Common Professional Exam (Law Society)
1 Diploma in Careers Guidance
1 Diploma in Management Studies
1 Certificate in Radio, Film and Television
1 writers' training course
1 Diploma in Movement and Dance

PERMANENT EMPLOYMENT: 64 graduates

9 teaching English abroad: *Greece (2); Italy*
(2); *Japan (2); China; Spain; Taiwan*
6 journalists: *Cambridge Town Crier; Centaur Communications; Exeter Express & Echo; Goodhead Publications; Scotland on Sunday; Tweeddale Press*
4 marketing/publicity trainees/assistants: *Applied Chemicals; Chatto & Windus; DHL; Cambridge Co-operative Society*
3 booksales assistants: *Waterstone & Company*
3 trainee account executives: *Ogilvy and Mather; Roundhouse Marketing; Simon Taylor Marketing*
3 housing administrators: *Anglia, Cambridge; Hounslow Council; unknown local authority*
3 publishing assistants: *Kensington West publications; Octopus Books; unknown publishing company*
3 trainee chartered accountants: *Deloitte Haskins & Sells; Touche Ross; unknown firm*
3 education administrators: *Bristol University; Anglia Higher Education College; college in Cambridge*
3 retail management trainees: *Galloway & Porter; Harrods; Heffers*
3 secretaries
2 teachers: *Cambridge Tutorial College*
2 disc-jockeys: *Devonair Radio; Hereford Local Radio*
2 theatre administrators: *Cambridge Arts Theatre; unknown theatre*
1 trainee computer programmer: *Hoskyns Group*
1 product manager: *Harcourt Brace Jovanowich*
1 trainee management consultant: *Arthur Andersen*
1 trainee insurance broker: *Alfred Blackmore*
1 banking trainee: *Bank of Scotland*
1 building society trainee: *Abbey National Building Society*
1 trainee tax inspector: *Inland Revenue*
1 research executive: *NOP Market Research*
1 nursing trainee: *National Health Service*
1 trainee interior designer: *Vickers*
1 purchasing trainee: *CEGB*
1 personnel management trainee: *British Telecom*
1 management trainee: *London Electricity Board*
1 police constable
1 voluntary worker

PLUS: 11 not available for employment; 15 in short-term employment; 2 overseas students leaving UK; 31 no information; 14 unemployed six months after graduating.

JOBS, CAREERS AND YOU

Physics

Examples of the destinations of 181 students who graduated from four universities and two polytechnics in 1988.

FURTHER FULL-TIME STUDY: 55 graduates

43 higher degree
8 Postgraduate Certificate in Education
1 first degree (LLB)
1 Diploma in Actuarial Science
1 Diploma in Production Engineering
1 Diploma in Surveying

PERMANENT EMPLOYMENT: 94 graduates

19 research and development scientists: *Ferranti (2); Marconi Defence Systems (2); Atomic Weapons Establishment; BP Chemicals; British Petroleum; Department of Transport; EEV; GP Inveresk Corporation; Hughes Microelectronics; ICI; Morganite Ceramic Fibres; National Nuclear Corporation; Philips Electronics; Royal Ordnance; See Factor (New York); T & N Technology; Thorn EMI*

17 engineers: *Motorola (3); British Aerospace (2); British Nuclear Fuels; British Steel; Computing Devices; Crosfield Electronics; Loss Prevention Council; Marconi Defence Systems; NCR;. NEC; National Semiconductor (UK); Plessey Microwave; Rolls-Royce & Associates; YARD*

4 trainee chartered accountants: *Binder Hamlyn (2); Deloitte Haskins & Sells (2)*

11 scientific officers: *Ministry of Defence (4); UKAEA (2); Admiralty Research Establishment; Atomic Energy Research Establishment; National Physical Laboratory; Royal Aerospace Establishments; Royal Armament Research and Development Establishment*

8 trainee computer programmers/software engineers: *IBM (2); British Rail; Comshare; Royal Bank of Scotland; STC; Software Sciences; unknown company*

5 sales/technical sales/marketing trainees: *Air Products; British Caribbean Citrus; Hewlett Packard; IBM; Metier Management Systems*

4 health/medical physicists: *National Health Service (3); British Nuclear Fuels*

4 trainee accountants: *British Petroleum (2); Commercial Union Assurance; TSB Commercial Holdings*

3 actuarial trainees: *FS Assurance; Guardian Royal Exchange; Royal Life*

3 management services trainees: *CEGB; NHS; Pilkington*

2 technologists: *Redfearn; unknown overseas company*

2 trainee systems analysts: *Easams; M4 Data*

2 systems engineers: *British Aerospace; Electronic Data Systems*

1 technical officer: *London Traffic Control Systems*

1 reactor physicist: *Rolls-Royce & Associates*

1 physicist/engineer: *British Antarctic Survey*

1 radio sound engineer: *BBC*

1 geophysical analyst: *Western Atlas*

1 external planning manager: *British Telecom*

1 trainee money broker: *Tullott and Tokyo Forex*

1 banking trainee: *TSB*

1 commercial trainee: *Lever Brothers*

1 management trainee: *British Steel*

PLUS: 3 not available for employment; 8 in short-term employment; 1 overseas student leaving UK; 8 no information; 12 unemployed six months after graduating.

From *What do Graduates do? 1990*

ASSIGNMENTS ▷ ▷ ▷ ▷ ▷ ▷ ▷ ▷

1 Let each member of your group choose a different one of the jobs listed. Imagine that you have taken that job and have been working for a few years. Take it in turns to explain the main advantages and disadvantages of doing the job to others in the group. Then suggest one way in which they might find out at first hand what it is like to do 'your' job.

2 Find areas of similarity and of difference between the two lists of job destinations of students. Why do you think some jobs are taken by both English and Physics students while other jobs are not? Consider this both from the point of view of the employees and what suits them, and from the point of view of employers.

COURSES AND SUBJECTS

Where do you start?

Let's say that you have decided that you want to carry on studying after school at college, polytechnic or university. You are getting on well enough with your sixth-form work to think that you could face more studying. You are finding enough of the work interesting to think that there may be some subjects you could face studying for several years. You want to gain higher qualifications so that you can hope for a better job in the career of your choice. But where do you start in order to find out about the different courses you could do?

Start by asking the right questions so that you stand a chance of finding out the answers you need to know.

Where should you study?

Before you finally decide where you are going to study, you should ask and satisfy yourself about the answers to the questions below.

About student life

- How many staff are there to how many students?
- How good are the facilities for study such as laboratories and libraries?
- How is the teaching organised in each department? (It will probably be very different from what you are used to)
- How big are the departments?
- How many staff?
- How is the work examined or assessed? (Again probably very different from what you are used to)
- What are the possibilities of doing a sandwich course?

About social life

- How many students are there?
- What are the relationships like between staff and students?
- Is there a good student health service?
- Is there a good careers service?
- What counselling and other advice services are on offer?
- What sporting facilities are there?
- What is the social life like?
- What is the proportion of men to women?

About the institution

- Where is the institution located in Great Britain?
- Is it in a town or what is the distance from the nearest town?
- How do you get to the town and how do you get to the institution?
- What proportion of students are accommodated on the campus?
- What are the rooms like?
- What are the catering arrangements?
- Are there shops, banks and similar facilities on the campus?
- What is the cost of living in the area? (It varies widely from one part of the country to another.)

From *What do Graduates do?* 1985

COURSES AND SUBJECTS

1 Choose a panel of three or four 'students' from your Tutor Group. Let the others pretend to be outsiders choosing whether to come to your own school or college sixth form. Arrange a question and answer session with the panel to find out what it is possible to study there. (Start by using some of the questions shown, as appropriate.)

2 Work through the list of questions shown and, in each case, write down whether you would expect to find the best answer to each question:
   (a) in the official prospectus,
   (b) by talking with present students,
   (c) by talking with staff,
   (d) some other way.

Preparing to make a decision

Where can you find out the answers to all your questions? Certainly there are some excellent source books, some of which are virtually essential references if you are not to make a dreadful mistake with your application. For example, you would be foolish to apply for a degree in Geology if you have not passed GCSE in Maths, or for Russian at Kent University where it's not offered as a subject. Your tutor will advise you on what to read and your careers department should be able to help you find useful books. Colleges, polytechnics and universities can advise you themselves, of course, and supply prospectuses for you to consider.

At some point, however, you will want to talk to people with first-hand experience of the place you are interested in, and the subjects you are thinking of choosing. Talk to your teachers and your tutor about this, go to 'open days' and meet students and staff. It is a good idea to look around somewhere before choosing to spend perhaps three years of your life there.

What do you need to do first, and what can you put off? Some deadlines are fixed for you, for instance by the UCCA and PCAS systems of application to university or polytechnic. But it is much better to organise your own research and decisions well in advance of final deadlines. Start in the summer, a full year earlier than the examinations, to visit colleges, meet staff and students, and read books that give a taste of what your chosen subject will be like. Then you will be well prepared for the decisions you must take in the examination year.

COURSES AND SUBJECTS

Deciding on courses

Do I want to continue studying?

Would I prefer to take a job, perhaps with day-release or training?

How well am I doing now? Could I manage more demanding work?

What subject to study?

What do I need to qualify or to lead on to my chosen career (if known)?

To university, polytechnic, college of further education or college of higher education?

What qualifications can I offer as likely GCE A level grades, etc? (for example, three grade Bs at A level with hard work, three Cs more likely).

What courses could I choose?

What is my 'short-list' of courses that I would like to do?

What are the minimum necessary qualifications for each course? (Check the *Compendium of University Entrance Requirements* or of *Advanced Courses*, etc.)

Check likely course offer (for example B,C,C at A level) from Brian Heap's *Degree course offers*.

Visit, perhaps an open day, and meet staff and students.

Read official (and unofficial) prospectuses.

How do I apply?

Decide on your entry for UCCA, PCAS, or colleges.

Read *How to Apply for Admission to a University, the UCCA Handbook* or *Polytechnic Courses Handbook* or another relevant handbook.

Complete details of interests, qualifications, etc.

Apply correctly, sensibly and in good time.

ASSIGNMENTS ▷ ▷ ▷ ▷ ▷ ▷ ▷ ▷

1 Find out from a willing member of staff her/his school-leaving qualifications (O and A levels – if he/she can remember!). Go and research, in your careers room or from other sources, to see what courses those qualifications might be suited to now. Draw up a short list of four courses that the member of staff should follow, and explain your recommendation to your tutor and the rest of the group.

2 In your groups, take it in turn to choose a particular course that can be studied at university, polytechnic or college. The other members of the group are allowed to ask up to twenty questions to try to guess what the course is called. The questions must be to do with what is studied in the course or what qualifications are needed to do it. Your tutor chairs the session.

WHAT NEXT?

Achieving that final goal

Some people find it easier to make the big decisions – 'I want to be a brain surgeon', 'I want to make a million', 'I want to get three As at A level' – than to make the smaller day-by-day decisions along the way. But it is only if you apply for the right courses with the right qualifications, or if you do a job well enough, or work really hard for the next GCSE assignment, that you can stay on the path to your final goal. You may be one of the many people who do not think in terms of 'final goals' anyway, but prefer to take each step along the way as it comes. If you do the right things, and do the best you can, you will end up where you want to be. In either case you must take decisions about what to apply for, and how to qualify for that job or course. You find yourself asking, time and again, 'What do I do next?'

ASSIGNMENTS ▷ ▷ ▷ ▷ ▷ ▷ ▷ ▷

1 What are your 'immediate goals' for this week? To what extent are they set by other people – teachers, your tutor, your parents/guardians – or by yourself?

2 Do you think people are (a) happier, (b) more successful if they can think in terms of more immediate goals instead of distant dreams?

3 Try to remember one major success that you have achieved and one great disappointment. What do you think you learned from each?

From school to college

Claire is a first-year student on a degree course in business studies. It's a four-year course and the third year is spent in a practical work placement. She chose business studies because it seemed relevant to a wide range of career openings and it seemed to her to be a 'useful subject'. Also it enabled her to study economics in more depth – the subject she studied at A level, with history.

Good groundwork

She wasn't totally sure at first whether business studies was the right course and there were so many applicants that she wasn't even invited for interview, but received an offer of a place on the strength of her written application. She did, though, manage to persuade her parents to spend a long weekend with her looking around the polytechnic she wanted to go to, and this at least gave her a chance to see the polytechnic, its buildings and the local town. She also knew one or two students who were already studying at the polytechnic and they were able to give her lots of useful bits of information and advice, particularly about the course she was applying for.

Hectic start

When Claire started the course, the first week was both hectic and sometimes confusing. Registration, getting her grant cheque, opening a bank account, meeting staff and students, all took place in the first few days. Luckily she had managed to get a place in a hall of residence and so at least she was spared the problem of finding somewhere to live! However, settling in to her new accommodation, finding her way around the campus, lecture rooms and the town all took time.

As far as the course was concerned, Claire was pleased with her choice; the staff in the department seemed friendly and the rest of the students – equal numbers of women and men – looked as though they were going to be fun to be with. Right from the start, though, she realised that study on a degree course was going to be very different from time spent in the sixth form. She was obviously going to need a lot more self motivation to get through the course, because the lecturers made little attempt to spoon-feed their students and this meant that every student had to be more independent in their approach. Also, in her lecture group there were nearly 50 students and this left little chance of individual attention during classes.

Exams

Now that she's nearing the end of her first year, Claire admits that the course hasn't all been plain sailing; the maths, stats and computing parts of the course have caused her some problems, but, having talked this over with tutors, she feels fairly confident of getting through her first-year exams, which represent the major hurdle facing most polytechnic and university students. She's made a determined effort to keep to a study timetable and not leave all her revision to the last moment.

Next year, she thinks the course will become more enjoyable, particularly when she starts to study real business problems and how to solve them! She would also like to get more involved in student issues, and in particular, to become student representative on the committee which plans her course, so that she can get to see 'behind the scenes' and find out how students can get their voice heard in what is taught and how it is taught.

Living away from home

Looking back, Claire admits that the year has changed her. It started with her feeling very unconfident about being able to cope living away from home and missing her family and friends. Gradually, however, she began to feel more at home, particularly through making friends and this, she feels, is the big plus point of being in a hall of residence – you seldom feel totally alone.

Her main worries have been about money. Claire always seemed to spend more than she should and never had enough to buy all the things she wanted. At the end of each term, her bank account has been overdrawn and she's had to rely on both financial help from parents and vacation jobs to get her account in order. Next year she plans to be more in control of her budgeting and keep a regular account of what she spends each week, especially as she's planning to share a rented house with some friends and they will have to do their own cooking and pay their own bills.

As for now, she's starting a vacation job after the exams are over, so that she has enough money for her holiday in France and Spain and has a well-earned break before the start of her next year of study.

From *What do Graduates do?* 1985

WHAT NEXT?

ASSIGNMENTS ▷ ▷ ▷ ▷ ▷ ▷ ▷ ▷

1 Make a list of the main steps Claire took in order to get on to her chosen course. To what extent have you done, or will you do, the same? Is there anything more that you could have suggested to Claire so that she could have made sure that her choice was a good one?

2 Imagine that you would like to do a course at the same polytechnic as Claire. Write a letter to her asking about that course, the staff, students, and life at the poly.

3 Claire seems pleased with her choice of course and polytechnic. Most students are. Why do you think people like Claire enjoy going on to university, polytechnic or college so much? What might she enjoy instead about taking a job after A levels?

LIFESTYLES AND INCOMES

What will you look for in a job?

Whether you start work as a sixth-form leaver or as a graduate with a degree, you will probably want a number of things. Money is important, of course, both when you first start to earn your living and, even more so, if you go on later to have a home, car, children and cat to support. Job satisfaction also matters, although different people find their satisfaction in very different ways. You may see your job as marking your position in society and giving you a certain way of life.

Some people drift into a job without being too clear why; others know that they are lucky to have any job they can get. But let us suppose that you have a choice, and can therefore think about what's on offer. The charts opposite show the earnings of employees in Britain in April 1984. Although the sums of money involved change from year to year, the major differences remain. Some people earn at least ten times as much as others. Is this fair? Why does it happen? Can you take it into account when choosing what you want to do?

ASSIGNMENTS ▷ ▷ ▷ ▷ ▷ ▷ ▷ ▷

1 Using all the graphs, compare the earnings and suggest reasons for the differences between:
   (a) men and women,
   (b) manual and non-manual employees,
   (c) medical practitioners, ambulancemen, and nurses and midwives.

2 Let each member of your Tutor Group take on one of the different jobs listed as occupation groups. Take it in turns to justify your own job and why you think you should be paid more for doing it compared with people doing different jobs. Use the data to help you.

3 Over the next forty or fifty years (your working lifetime) there will be major changes in technical progress, social organisation, and job prospects. How would you expect these changes to affect the main differences in earning shown in the charts?

Distribution of gross weekly earnings[1], April 1984

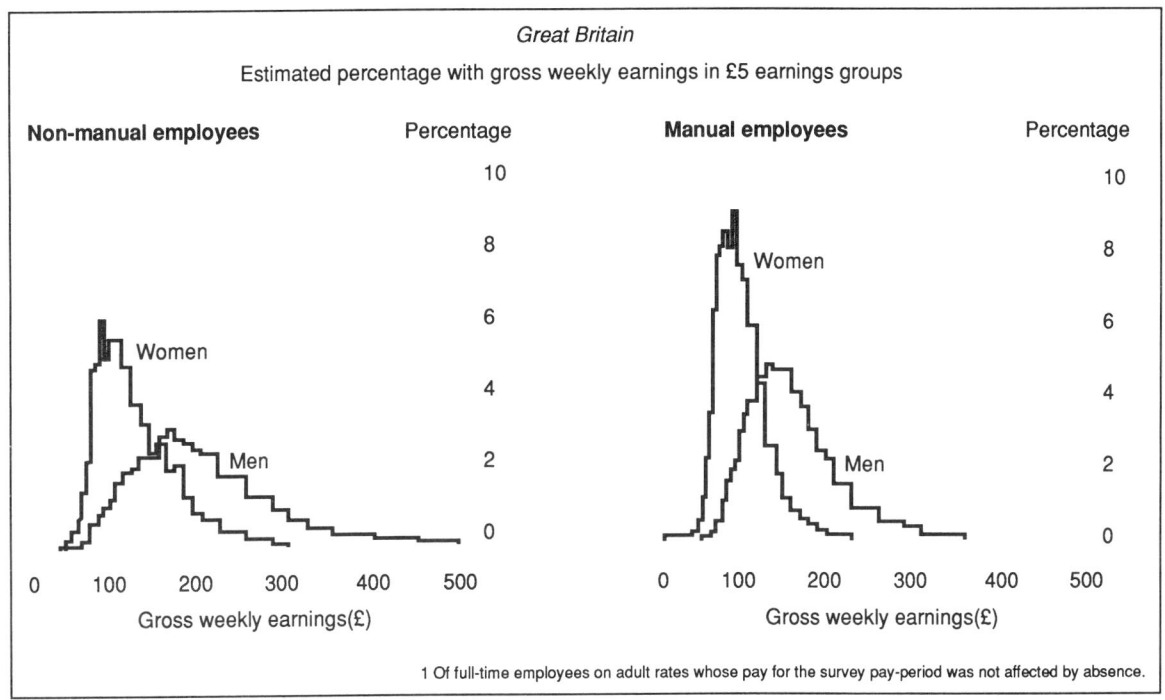

Great Britain

Estimated percentage with gross weekly earnings in £5 earnings groups

Non-manual employees Percentage

Manual employees Percentage

Women

Men

Gross weekly earnings(£)

1 Of full-time employees on adult rates whose pay for the survey pay-period was not affected by absence.

Average gross weekly earnings[1] of full-time employees[2] in selected occupation groups, April 1984: by sex

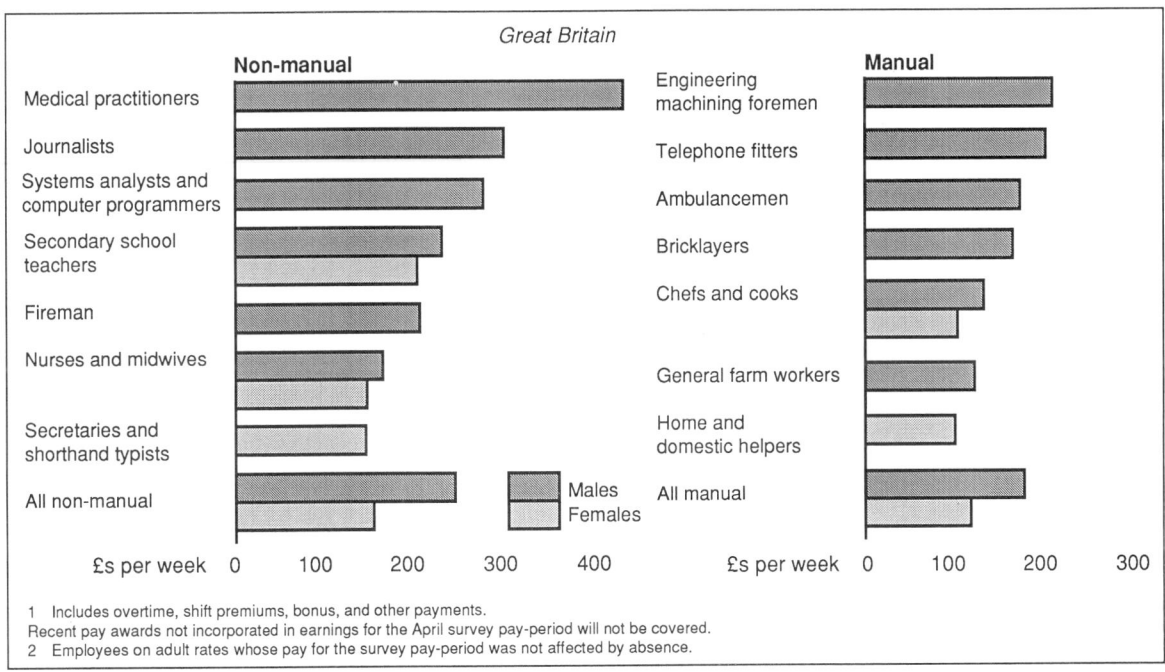

Great Britain

Non-manual

Medical practitioners
Journalists
Systems analysts and computer programmers
Secondary school teachers
Fireman
Nurses and midwives
Secretaries and shorthand typists
All non-manual

£s per week

Manual

Engineering machining foremen
Telephone fitters
Ambulancemen
Bricklayers
Chefs and cooks
General farm workers
Home and domestic helpers
All manual

£s per week

Males
Females

1 Includes overtime, shift premiums, bonus, and other payments.
Recent pay awards not incorporated in earnings for the April survey pay-period will not be covered.
2 Employees on adult rates whose pay for the survey pay-period was not affected by absence.

From *Social Trends*, HMSO, 1986

Profit and loss

Nick Baker talks to the international money dealer who gave up £150,000 a year to become a nursery teacher.

Last May, Soo Pickett changed the tools of her trade. Until then, they were the telephone and the computer. Now, they are building blocks, counting beads and the sandpaper letters used in Montessori nursery education.

As a successful floating rate note or Eurobond dealer with the Bank of America, it wasn't remarkable if $100 million crossed her desk in a day. Dealers at her level could earn between £100,000 and £150,000 a year.

Now she is on the one-year nursery teachers' course at the London Montessori Centre and enjoying being a student again, particularly the practical teaching experience. After she has taught for a while she hopes to open a nursery school of her own, investing what's left of her earnings in what she refers to as "the casino" – the Bank of America dealing room. Not that she's assured of having a lot of that money left after a few years' experience in a profession where salaries rarely top £5,000. However, she is optimistic about her future in education and, after six months' study, entirely committed to the Montessori method.

After training as a translator at the French Institute in London, she went into stockbroking as a "translator-secretary-dogsbody", and thence into the heady world of investment banking, ending up as one of the few women in the hot seats of the Bank of America dealing room. The job she left last year at the age of 30 (having started at 25) was essentially dealing in international debt, buying and selling to commercial and national banks. She likens the dealing room to a casino because dealers are often in a position of losing money they don't really have.

"You're dealing with chips," she says. "At the end of the day you hope you've got it all back and made a profit." Her table limits were a closely guarded secret between her and her employer. The million dollar deals she made every day were settled by word of mouth over an international telephone line. On the freewheeling Eurobond market, a dealer's word is her bond.

The dramatic career change came about as the result of numerous factors. Soo Pickett didn't suffer the dramatic "burn out" some city whizz kids undergo after a relatively short dealing career on the moneymarkets. She left with her professional reputation intact.

But the years of arriving at her desk at 7.15 am and scarcely leaving it until 12 hours later (sometimes with the prospect of more telephoning at home during the night) exhausted the necessary supply of adrenalin, and closed off the rest of the world.

The dealing room was a world apart from the average nursery school – a world which keeps a team of British Telecom engineers employed replacing phones that have been smashed down in anger or frustration, a world of ambitious young professionals who eat, sleep and breathe the money markets, flopping into their jacuzzis at the weekend to try to recharge the batteries.

One trap that Soo Pickett carefully avoided was that of accepting a large preferential rate mortgage from her employer – fine when you're an employee but hard to extricate yourself from when you leave – and she never went in for the jacuzzi and Porsche image.

At the point of leaving banking, she had no idea what she wanted to do, other than sleep for a month: "I was a lopsided person when I left. I knew an awful lot about banking, but never had time for anything else. The last time I'd read a good book was when I was at college. I needed something that could give me a radically different perspective on life."

Teaching certainly fitted the bill, but she was wary of investing the time needed to become qualified for state teaching and unsure whether she could cope with a life of what for her would be comparative poverty. On the other hand, she'd been nagged by a social conscience which she'd hitherto only been able to exercise by squeezing in some fund-raising for the World Wildlife Fund and by "paying an awful lot of tax". When she saw the benefits a two-year-old acquaintance was getting from Montessori education, and found out that the nursery training was only a year, she decided that was the way forward.

There were some reservations. Soo Pickett dislikes the privilege attached to the private nature of Montessori (in London, a mornings-only term will cost parents about £200) and she would welcome the idea of schools taking on more non-fee payers. She'd also like to see Montessori methods being taken on in mainstream education. But by and large, she's enthusiastic about her new career. However, she does find that at times the pressures of working with lively young children can be almost as great as those dealing with international financiers.

"It's a tiredness I can regenerate from," she says. It's certainly a different tiredness to the drained feeling after a day in the dealing room, eyes glued to a computer screen, brain buzzing with on the spot calculations and nerves jangling to the tune of breaking phones.

From *The Times Educational Supplement*, 11 April 1986

LIFESTYLES AND INCOME

ASSIGNMENTS ▷ ▷ ▷ ▷ ▷ ▷ ▷ ▷

1 Make out a list for Soo Pickett for and against her decision to leave money dealing. How different might her decision have been at the ages of twenty, or forty, do you think?

2 Choose roles so that half your group pretend to be money dealers and the other half nursery teachers. Take turns to explain the main advantages of your 'own' job and the lifestyle associated with it. As a conclusion ask your own tutor to choose one job or the other on the balance of the argument.

3 Would you prefer to be **married** to a money dealer or a nursery teacher? Choose one way or the other and then write a letter to a monthly magazine complaining about your lot.

APPLYING FOR COURSES

Questions

1 'I don't need to plough through all the individual university, polytechnic and college prospectuses, I can use *Which Degree?*.'

TRUE/FALSE

2 Apart from the use of language, what do the following degree subjects have in common?

Philosophy
Celtic studies
Communication and media studies
Linguistics

3 Has someone tried to put you off with statements like these?

'There's only one course for Canadian studies isn't there? And I've been turned down.'

TRUE/FALSE

'You've hardly any choice if you want to study Hebrew.'

TRUE/FALSE

'It's easy if you want to be a conference interpreter, you can choose any modern language course.'

TRUE/FALSE

'You have to study Shakespeare and the Elizabethans in all English courses and I don't want to.'

TRUE/FALSE

4 Few institutions insist on A level history as an entrance requirement for history courses.

TRUE/FALSE

A level art is not essential for entry to a degree course in art and design.

TRUE/FALSE

5 University courses are carefully named and courses with similar titles invariably have very similar contents.

TRUE/FALSE

6 Polytechnics provide few courses in the following:

Classics	TRUE/FALSE
Theology	TRUE/FALSE
History	TRUE/FALSE
Spanish	TRUE/FALSE
Philosophy	TRUE/FALSE

7 In joint honours courses, the individual courses are always designed with a view to complementing each other.

TRUE/FALSE

8 Spot the odd man out:
   (i) Batik
   (ii) Silk screen printing
   (iii) Constructivism
   (iv) Mosaic
   (v) Orthographic

9 Which of the following occupations can be entered with an arts degree?
   (a) HM factory inspector
   (b) Computer programmer
   (c) Occupational therapist
   (d) Radiographer
   (e) Research officer (Civil Service)

10 In many language courses, a choice of optional or subsidiary courses is required at the start of the first year.

TRUE/FALSE

From G. Carpenter, *Which Degree 1985*, VNU Business Publications, 1985

ASSIGNMENTS ▷ ▷ ▷ ▷ ▷ ▷ ▷ ▷

Try to answer the above questions about degree courses. Then check the answers given opposite. (For further details refer to the publication.)

APPLYING FOR COURSES

Answers

1 FALSE. *Which Degree?* has been carefully designed to help you narrow the field but you should still consult the individual prospectuses of the colleges you choose.

2 They are all subjects which are not traditionally studied at school.

3 TRUE, FALSE, TRUE, FALSE. This is the kind of general information you will find in the useful *course introductions* to each subject.

4 TRUE. History would appear to be the most logical requirement since it is an academic rather than a practical or technical subject like art. Some institutions prefer it, but few demand it.
   TRUE. Art is not an essential requirement for all courses.
   This is the kind of information which you will find in the *entrance requirements* section accompanying each subject area.

5 FALSE. A careful investigation of the *course telegrams* sent in by the institutions to describe their courses will cure you of any doubt on this one

6 TRUE, TRUE, FALSE, FALSE, FALSE. Although there are very few single subject courses in these subjects at polytechnics, history, Spanish and philosophy can be taken in quite a number of combined studies programmes. Don't forget to look at the *joint courses* section as well as *single subjects*.

7 FALSE. Many seek to bridge the gap in a meaningful way but one should not rely on this. There are still many courses where the subjects are unrelated and/or taught in different schools or departments creating problems for timetables and loyalties.

8 Mosaic doesn't just mean a picture made up of small pieces of stone. It's also a theological term and the remainder are terms from creative art.
   Despite individual course differences, some technical terms are widely used in course descriptions. Be sure to consult the glossary of *common terms* presented in each subject area.

9 They may all be entered with an arts degree. Students are often surprised at the range of occupations which may be entered after such courses, their value as an intellectual training.

10 TRUE. Although most option choices are made at a later stage of a course, there are still many courses where first year options are required.

Filling in the application forms

The first step in applying for educational courses after leaving school is to find out about all the possibilities that interest you. The next is to compare your qualifications, or what you expect them to be, with the requirements for each course. This gives you the chance to 'shop around', seeing what you can find. If your qualifications are strong you have a 'lot of money to spend' so to speak and can afford a higher 'priced' course with higher entrance requirements. Then, in the end, you must make your decisions, and fill in the application forms.

Universities and polytechnics have their own application forms through the UCCA and PCAS systems respectively. This cuts down repeated form-filling, but cuts down your choice as well. You must choose a few courses you would like to follow, and be careful to include those with requirements you could hope to meet both at best, and at worst. Obviously you must read the forms carefully: if asked to give details of all exams taken whatever the result, you must

APPLYING FOR COURSES

do so; if asked to include payment, or to 'print in black ink', you must do so!

Some parts of application forms, however, are much more difficult to respond to. You may be asked to give details of your 'interests, activities and other relevant information' or to explain 'why you are applying for each particular course'. It is worth practising your answers to these questions, and asking advice from your tutor when you have done so.

A typical question

'What are your personal interests and activities? Give details of any other experience relevant to this course.'

I read quite a lot, mainly science fiction and 'New Musical Express' and go out to gigs and parties. I like music, mainly heavy metal, and I play and guitar in a band. I like travelling and holidays in the South of France. I work in the local supermarket on Saturdays.

Sport - Badminton (school captain), swimming (local club), jogging (sponsored runs for charity).

Post of responsibility - deputy chairperson of school sixth-form social committee.

Interests - music: playing guitar and running my own band; pop music; light reading; Asimov and Sharpe; travel; current affairs.

Relevant experience - business methods from part-time work in local retailers; foreign language conversation on French exchange.

ASSIGNMENTS ▷ ▷ ▷ ▷ ▷ ▷ ▷ ▷

1 Imagine that you are an admissions tutor at a university. Which one of the above applications would impress you most favourably? Give your reasons, and suggest lines of questioning at interviews.

2 Write your own answer to the 'typical question'. Set up interviews in your Tutor Group, with one person as an admissions tutor, asking questions on the basis of the other person's written answer. The others in the group should observe and comment on particular strengths or weaknesses in the written and interview answers.

APPLYING FOR JOBS

At some stage of your life, you will have days dominated by writing letters applying for jobs or courses. It is not an easy task, but it is a very important one because your letter is the first impression you make on a future employer.

OFFICE JUNIOR

Opportunity to start work in a thriving estate agency. Interesting variety of work plus training in sales and estimating.
Suit young, dynamic, hard working school leaver or graduate.
Basic salary plus generous commission.

Write to: Sita Griffith,
Griffith Estate Agency,
111 Hanger Lane,
Southfield SO9 1QX

Which letter makes the best impression?

15 Curzon Road
Southfield
SO2 9BZ

Mr S. Griffith,
Griffiths Estate Agency,
111 Hanger Lane
Southfield SO9 1QX.

Dear Sir,
    I saw your advertisement in The Gazette last week and am interested in applying. My uncle is an estate agent and I have helped in his office during holidays. He is James Glynde of Glynde and Tower Ltd. He says he will act as a referee for me. My school will be the other referee, if you write to Mrs Smith, the Sixth Form Co-ordinator.
    I have 5 GCSEs and am now studying three A levels in Geography, History and Sociology. My parents have made me fill in UCCA forms but I would like to start work instead.
    I hope to hear from you soon.
            Yours sincerely,
            Janet Peters

APPLYING FOR JOBS

40 Selby Road
Southfield
6.7.90

Dear Ms Griffith,
I would like to apply for the job of office Junior. I am leaving school this summer and I hope to have good passes in Maths, English and Commerce. I have a Saturday job this year in the newsagents across the road from you and I have always liked the look of your office. I could easily come in to see you.
Thank you.
Yours sincerely,
Lucy James

Mr. S. Griffiths,
Griffiths Estate Ag.
111 Hanger Lane
SO9 1QX.

72 Barnfield Ave,
Southfield

Dear Mr Griffiths,
Re. Post of Office Junior
I am writing to apply for the above post as advertised in the Gazette. I would like to work in an estate agency because I like working with people. I am a scout and used to being responsible and hard working. I am captain of swimming at school so I hope I could be called 'dynamic' too!
My mother is now on her own and I want to work locally to keep an eye on her. I would be able to start work at the beginning of August.
I hope you will consider me for an interview.
Yours faithfully,
Winston Ngomi

ASSIGNMENTS ▷ ▷ ▷ ▷ ▷ ▷ ▷ ▷

1 What are the good and bad points in each letter?

2 Choose two of these applicants to interview. Why did you select them?

3 There are at least eight points to include in a good letter of application. See if you can work out what these are.

4 Write your own letter of application for the same post.

PREPARING A CURRICULUM VITAE

Curriculum Vitae is Latin for the 'course of life'. It is most likely that you will not need such a statement for the next few years, but it might be useful to prepare your own now before you start applying for courses and jobs. Then you could keep it to add to, photocopy and send as a general statement about yourself. Always write a covering letter that is relevant to the particular recipient.

CURRICULUM VITAE

<u>Name:</u> SARAH WONDERFUL (MISS)
<u>Home address:</u> 20 ANY ROAD, SOMETOWN, HERESHIRE HR2 3ZZ
<u>Phone:</u> 007-12345
<u>College address:</u> EGGHEAD HALL, THERESHIRE
<u>Phone:</u> 321-99199
<u>Marital status:</u> SINGLE   <u>Nationality:</u> BRITISH
<u>Date of birth:</u> 18/4/62   <u>Age:</u> 22

EDUCATION
<u>Secondary:</u> SOMETOWN HIGH SCHOOL 1973-1980
<u>University:</u> EGGHEAD HALL, THERESHIRE UNIVERSITY 1980-1984
<u>Academic qualifications:</u>
<u>O levels:</u> ENGLISH LANGUAGE, FRENCH, HISTORY, MATHS, PHYSICS
<u>A levels:</u> FRENCH (B), MATHS (E), PHYSICS (A)
<u>BA Hons Degree:</u> FRENCH (2:2)

EMPLOYMENT
Summer 1983   HERESHIRE BOOKSTORE   SALES ASSISTANT
Summer 1982   FRENCH SUNNYTOURS   TOUR COURIER
Winter 1981   HERESHIRE BAKERY   SALES ASSISTANT

ADDITIONAL INFORMATION
TYPING: 30 wpm CURRENT DRIVING LICENCE

OTHER INTERESTS
ACTING, NETBALL (UNIVERSITY 2ND TEAM), PRESIDENT OF EGGHEAD HALL
YOUNG LIBERALS, VOLUNTARY WORK AT HERESHIRE HOSPITAL

REFEREES
<u>Academic:</u> MR TOM BRAIN, FRENCH TUTOR, EGGHEAD HALL, THERESHIRE
<u>Character:</u> MRS JANE GOOD, DIRECTOR, FRENCH SUNNYTOURS, THERESHIRE

From *The Sunday Times Good Career Guide*, Grafton Books, 1985

PREPARING A CURRICULUM VITAE

Read this profile of David Bintley so that you
can answer the assignment questions which
follow it.

PROFILE OF DAVID BINTLEY, BRITAIN'S BRIGHTEST YOUNG CHOREOGRAPHER

David Bintley was born in Huddersfield and attended the Audrey Spencer
School before joining The Royal Ballet School. After a resounding success as
Dr Coppelius in The School's Performance of *Coppelia* in June 1976, he
joined Sadler's Wells Royal Ballet in September of that year.

At the age of twenty, in 1978, he created *The Outsider* becoming one of
the youngest choreographers ever to create a work for Sadler's Wells Royal
Ballet; *Meadow of Proverbs* followed in March 1979 and *Punch and the Street
Party* was premiered later that year at the Edinburgh International Festival.

In 1980, he created his first work for The Royal Ballet, *Adieu*, and two
further works for Sadler's Wells Royal Ballet, *Homage to Chopin* and *Polonia*.
1981 saw the premiere of *Night Moves* (for Sadler's Wells Royal Ballet)
followed, in 1982, by his first three-act work *The Swan of Tuonela*. Following
the latter successes, Bintley was appointed Company Choreographer of
Sadler's Wells Royal Ballet in April 1983. In September of that year, he
created *Choros* for Sadler's Wells Royal Ballet, and, only three months later,
premiered his second work for The Royal Ballet, *Consort Lessons*. These two
ballets won Bintley the London Standard Ballet Award for 1983.

Metamorphosis was premiered by Sadler's Wells Royal Ballet in April 1984.
Young Apollo his third work for The Royal Ballet, was premiered in November
that year.

Subsequently, Bintley revived a 1979 ballet, originally created at the request
of Vyvyan Lorrayne, adding a new work to it and calling the two together
Flowers of the Forest (for Sadler's Wells Royal Ballet). This was premiered in
June 1985 and was followed by another work for The Royal Ballet, *The Sons
of Horus*, in October.

The Snow Queen, David Bintley's second full-length work for Sadler's Wells
Royal Ballet, was premiered on 28 April 1986. *Galanteries*, for The Royal
Ballet, was premiered in July 1986 as part of the Company's visit to Expo '86
and opened the 1986/87 season at the Royal Opera House. Bintley was also
appointed Resident Choreographer of The Royal Ballet from the beginning of
that season. Since then he has choreographed a new one-act work, *Allegri
Diversi* for Sadler's Wells Royal Ballet (premiered at Sadler's Wells Theatre in
January 1987) the waltz for Anthony Dowell's new production of *Swan Lake*
(March 1987), and three new one-act works for The Royal Ballet, *'Still Life' at
the Peguin Cafe* (March 1988), *The Trial of Prometheus* (October 1988) and
The Spirit of Fugue (November 1988). *'Still Life' at the Penguin Cafe* won the
1988 Manchester Evening News Award for Dance. Most recently, he has
choreographed a new full-length ballet for Sadler's Wells Royal Ballet,

PREPARING A CURRICULUM VITAE

Hobsons's Choice, premiered at the Royal Opera House in February 1989 as a two-act ballet.

David Bintley is also a Principal Dancer of The Royal Ballet and a very accomplished dramatic dancer and mime artist. Since joining The Royal Ballet, his roles have included Bottom in Ashton's *The Dream* and Widow Simone in *La Fille mal Gardée*, also by Sir Frederick Ashton (both previously danced with Sadler's Wells Royal Ballet), the Short Ugly Sister in *Cinderella*, Steuart-Powell in *Enigma Variations* and Drosselmeyer in *The Nutcracker*. Other roles in his repertoire for Sadler's Wells Royal Ballet include Alain (*La Fille mal Gardée*), Gremio (*The Taming of the Shrew*), the Red King (*Checkmate*), Doctor Coppelius (*Coppelia*) and the title role in *Petruschka* for which he was awarded the 1984 Laurence Olivier Award for Dance.

Royal Ballet Press Office, September 1989

ASSIGNMENTS ▷ ▷ ▷ ▷ ▷ ▷ ▷ ▷

1 After you have studied Sarah Wonderful's CV draw up one for David Bintley.

2 What do you notice is missing from Sarah Wonderful's CV? How might you get across this information to a prospective employer or course organiser?

3 Now write (a) your own CV, and (b) a letter to accompany the CV to a prospective employer or course organiser.

INTERVIEW TECHNIQUES

It is very likely that in the next few years you will be given an interview. After an application letter an interview is the only opportunity you have to present yourself as suitable for the particular course or work you wish to do. It is therefore important that you are as well prepared as possible for the situation. The more practice you have had, the less nerve-racking the interview should be.

Juliet Bravo: Expectations

Jean is at her desk with Hannah sitting opposite, straight backed, hands neatly folded on her lap.
Jean is leafing through her file.

JEAN	So you worked in an office originally?
HANNAH	Yes, ma'am.
JEAN	Doing what?
HANNAH	Typing, filing. General office dogsbody. It bored me rigid.
JEAN	(*a small smile*) And you decided police work wouldn't?
HANNAH	I wanted to do something a little more demanding than pounding a typewriter.

That unnerving confidence is there again.
Jean turns a page of the file.

JEAN   I see you specially asked for this attachment? (*She looks at Hannah*) Why here, in particular?

HANNAH   (*with disconcerting frankness*) Because of you.

Jean stares at her, puzzled.

You came to the training school, gave us a talk about women's integration in the force, how it's been for the good, how women still have to try twice as hard to prove themselves, but they could do it if they had the determination . . .

It comes out a like a set speech she's pre-rehearsed for the occasion.
Jean cuts in on it.

JEAN   I obviously made an impression.

HANNAH   You did.

Again, that frank confidence.
She's treating Jean as an equal, or even as if she is the one doing the interviewing.

JEAN   (*mildly*) And you thought . . . by asking for this posting . . . that you'd get . . . preferential treatment?

Hannah wasn't expecting this, it wasn't part of the plan.

HANNAH Not at all . . . why d'you say that?

JEAN It's one interpretation . . .

Hannah regards her a moment, when she speaks her tone is defiantly defensive suddenly.

HANNAH I simply wanted to work under someone I admired and respected. Is there anything wrong with that?

JEAN That's important to you?

HANNAH Of course, isn't it to you?

Jean smiles slightly again but doesn't reply.
She's quite enjoying the interview.

JEAN And supposing I don't live up to your expectations, what then? (*The camera concentrates on Hannah's face, puzzled.*) What I'm saying is, giving a lecture on theory is one thing, putting it into practice is another . . . You might not find that relaxed performance you saw me give at the training school applies here . . . it doesn't.

HANNAH (*defensive again*) You asked me why I applied for this attachment and I've told you the reason . . .

JEAN And I'm simply suggesting there might be more appropriate ones . . . the job is what counts, not the people who do it.

There's a pause.

HANNAH Yes, ma'am.

Her tone is now starkly formal, as if resenting the authority in Jean's tone.

JEAN I . . . don't get the feeling I've explained myself too well.

HANNAH Oh, I think I understand what you're saying, ma'am.

From Alison Leake (ed), *Juliet Bravo*, Longman, 1983

ASSIGNMENTS ▷ ▷ ▷ ▷ ▷ ▷ ▷ ▷

1 What has gone wrong with the interview from this *Juliet Bravo* script?

2 Identify from the script the following styles of speech usually adopted by an interviewer:
- contact question
- opinion-seeking question
- probe question
- supportive statement
- 'pregnant' pause
- straight interrogative
- extension question to prompt a fuller answer
- hypothetical question
- rhetorical question

3 Now give an alternative for each to the ones used in the script. What is the point of each type of question?

INTERVIEW TECHNIQUES

Bad interviewees . . .

- arrive late
- look scruffy
- have tried to be too trendy
- talk too loudly
- throw their weight about
- sniff
- giggle
- smoke
- chew gum
- smell of alcohol, drugs or garlic
- loll in their chairs
- don't answer the questions
- don't know why they want the job
- don't speak clearly
- expect the employer or admissions tutor to be a mind-reader
- can't remember what they put on their application form
- get muddled over dates and places
- expect the interviewer to be bowled over by their paper qualifications
- 'take over' the interview.

From *What do Graduates do?* 1985

ASSIGNMENTS ▷ ▷ ▷ ▷ ▷ ▷ ▷ ▷

1 Work in pairs to set up an interview for a course or job of your choice.

Interviewer. Look at the style of an interviewer again in the extract from *Juliet Bravo*, then prepare other relevant questions to ask, for example:

- Tell me about your present work or studies.
- What attracts you to this course or job?
- What qualities do you think you could bring to the course or job?

Interviewee: Prepare:

- answers to the above questions;
- questions you want answered about the course or job;
- so that you can make a good impression.

2 Role-play your interview in front of either a video camera or another pair/group. Be ready to offer and accept criticism.

3 Study the list on 'Bad interviewees'. Now prepare a list entitled 'Good interviewees'.

TIME OUT

Time between school and college

By the time you leave the sixth form of your school or college you will probably have spent thirteen years or so in full-time education. That's quite a sentence! Some people feel by then that they deserve time off for good behaviour – or rather 'time out' between school and further education or a job. This needs to be seen positively if it is to be a success. Ask yourself what you can **do** with the time rather than just 'take a break from studying'. Ask yourself where you can **go** rather than just 'not straight on to college' or whatever. And ask yourself what time out can give you, or what you can give of yourself to make it time well spent.

ASSIGNMENTS ▷ ▷ ▷ ▷ ▷ ▷ ▷ ▷

1 Suppose that you can apply for a grant for taking one year away from full-time education. Write a short proposal justifying your intended use of that time and money – as a tramp.

2 Let your tutor, or one member of your Tutor Group, pretend to be the tramp in the cartoon. Everyone else in the group is a student in full-time education; try to convince the tramp about what he/she is missing in a free discussion.

Useful alternatives

James Constable, a first-year student of maths and physical education at Loughborough University, spent three months last year working as a volunteer with severely handicapped people in a Cheshire Home. Then he took a series of factory jobs in order to finance two overseas trips to the United States and France.

James took what is known as a 'year out' or 'gap year'. Some of this year's sixth-formers have already decided to do the same and others may be wondering whether to follow suit.

Is it a good idea? Parents often worry that their offspring may lose the motivation for higher education in the intervening year. Young people are sometimes afraid that their university or polytechnic might not approve. Undoubtedly, some students do 'go off the boil' but they could well be the ones who would have dropped out in the first term.

Genuine motivation rarely disappears in one year. Admittedly, some lecturers, particularly those in maths departments, are against the idea. James readily admits to finding the maths contents of his course hard after a year's break.

Happily for young people contemplating the idea, few admissions officers now react negatively to it and most think it beneficial. They feel students on the whole come up more motivated and more mature. Reading University some time ago followed up a group of students who had entered the university after a gap year. Some admitted to initial problems in settling down – even to finding the other students 'childish' – but none performed less well academically than expected.

James agrees with all these points. The difficulty with maths is, he says, far outweighed by the positive things he has gained. He is much more independent and thinks he has gained from his travels. He points out that he comes from a small town in Hampshire and had been away before only on organized college trips. Now, he has met very different kinds of people and has learned, unlike some of his contemporaries, to handle his finances. 'I saw them going mad when their grant cheques arrived. They'd never had to budget before.'

Employers when interviewing graduates are usually interested in previous work experience, particularly if relevant, and in candidates who have done something interesting or unusual.

What to do in a year out can be a problem. Admissions staff as well as employers like evidence of something constructive. Definitions of this vary. Some think highly of voluntary work; some of paid employment. Some approve of time spent in acquiring an additional skill such as a language; others have no objection to foreign travel. The only safe thing to do is contact the proposed institution, outline plans, and ask what they think.

It is important to plan ahead. What no one regards as constructive is a year spent adding to the unemployment figures because no job materialized. It is no good deferring a higher education place and then finding oneself with nothing to do. James started to plan his year well in advance, arranging voluntary work first, and subsequently took whatever temporary jobs were available.

James Constable arranged his own placement and thoroughly enjoyed it, even though he was thrown in at the deep end. He got to know residents, permanent staff and other volunteers well. He shared the residents' lives and helped with everything from feeding, bathing and personal care to hobbies, outings and domestic work. Since leaving, he has been back to attend the wedding of two residents. His year turned into a very good combination of social work, earning money and enjoying foreign travel.

Siobhan Boxall, now at Surrey University doing a nursing degree, spent last year in Pakistan, working with eight other volunteers sent to teach English in a language teaching centre. There was initial culture shock, particularly for the three girls who had to adapt quickly to the restrictions imposed on them – living in a separate house with a 'chaperone', and only allowed to teach females. It was a totally different lifestyle.

'We had to relearn the art of conversation in the evenings,' she says. 'I suppose we amused ourselves in the ways we did here before television.' Local people though were kind. The girls conformed, wearing local dress and covering their heads in public. As a result they were often invited into homes and became popular wedding guests.

Travelling was not easy, cinema visits forbidden and eating in restaurants had to be done in curtained off areas. But they did manage to go out – always in a group – with the male volunteers, and the organization encouraged them to meet at weekends with other groups. Towards the end of the year they managed a trip to India. Siobhan had a marvellous year, but did feel a kind of reverse culture shock for several weeks after her return.

The organization provided orientation and teaching method courses, and as is the usual practice, made their travel and accommodation arrangements. It also paid them an allowance, generous by local standards, out of which they had to buy their food.

Travel broadens the mind, the saying goes, and most students who spend time abroad between A levels and higher education claim to benefit. Thinking back to her Pakistan experience, Siobhan says that it helped her to grow up. She learned a lot about herself; how to work with other people; and how to manage money. Some of her university friends were surprised at the end of their first term when, instead of being overdrawn, she had actually saved.

From Beryl Dixon in *The Times*, 5 May and 12 May 1986

ASSIGNMENTS ▷ ▷ ▷ ▷ ▷ ▷ ▷ ▷

1 List the steps that James Constable took to prepare his 'year out'. Do you think the experiences of James and Siobhan would have been as successful if they had exchanged roles?

2 Make out a short list of four or five ways in which you would most like to use a year out of full-time education. Include some where money is no object, some that are realistic, some at home, but most living away – possibly in other countries.

3 Choose a panel of three from your Tutor Group to act as admissions staff at university, polytechnic or college. Take turns to put your preferred proposal to them explaining why you want to spend a year 'out' in that way. Let them conduct the interview to check that your ideas are positive and well-prepared.

Answers to questions on page 113	
1 T	6 T
2 T	7 F
3 F	8 T
4 F	9 T
5 T	10 F

Acknowledgements

We are grateful to the following for permission to reproduce copyright material:

The Author, Nick Baker for an extract from his article 'Profit and Loss' in *The Times Educational Supplement* 11.4.86; BBC Publications for an adapted extract from 'Scene 105' in *The Two of Us* by Leslie Stewart, BBC Filmscript 1987; University of Cambridge Local Examinations Syndicate for questions 3, 4, 7, 8, 10, 11, 12, 13 & 14 from '*A' Level General Studies Papers* 1, 2 & 3 Summer 1982; the Author, Geoffrey Cannon for an extract from his article 'The Food Scandal' in *The Times* 13.6.84; the Author, Anthony W. Clare for an extract from his article 'Sex and Politics' in *The Sunday Times* 23.3.86; Ewan Macnaughton Associates on behalf of The Daily Telegraph plc for extracts from the articles 'Marriage still firmly rooted', 'Flowers ease the pain for mother who reported son' by A. J. McIlroy & 'The conflicting ideals of life without stress' by Lesley Garner in *The Daily Telegraph* 27.4.88, 20.6.88 & 27.4.88 © The Daily Telegraph plc; the Author, Beryl Dixon for extract entitled 'Useful Alternatives' based on her articles in *The Times* 5.5.86 & 12.5.86; The Hartford Courant for an extract from the article 'Mom is outnumbered' by Barbara Roessner reprinted in *International Herald Tribune* 19.4.88; Hobsons Publishing plc for extracts from *What Do Graduates Do?* © 1985 & 1990 by the Association of Graduate Careers Advisory Services, IPC Magazines Ltd for an extract from the article 'When a Child Steals' in *Woman* 24.4.71; Jay Landesman for the poem 'Do a Dance for Daddy' by Fran Landesman from *Is it Overcrowded in Heaven?*, Golden Handshake 1981; Methuen London for an extract from *Educating Rita* by Willy Russell (Longman Study Text edition); Authors' Agents for poem 'Five Years Old' by Adrian Mitchell from *For Beauty Douglas (Collected poems 1953–1979)* Allison & Busby Ltd by permission of the Peters, Fraser & Dunlop Group Ltd Neither this nor any other of Adrian Mitchell's poems are to be used in connection with any examination whatsoever; the Author, Kate McEwan for an extract from her *Ealing Walkabout;* Authors' Agents for an extract from 'Expectations' script by Paula Milne in *Juliet Bravo* (Longman Imprint Books) © Paula Milne; The Newpoint Publishing Co Ltd for an extract from *Which Degree* 1985 by G. Carpenter; The Observer Ltd for the article 'She is a slag, he is a stud' in The *Observer* 15.6.86; Penguin Books Ltd for article 'The Least Successful Animal Rescue' from *The Book of Heroic Failures* by Stephen Pile (Viking, 1989) © Stephen Pile, 1979; Quiller Press Ltd for an extract from *Shinwell Talking* by John Doxat (Quiller Press, 1984); the Author, Lee Rodwell for extracts from her articles 'A Step Not Taken Lightly' ('The pitfalls and how to avoid them') & 'Does He Deserve It?' in *The Times* 27.6.86 & 17.6.88; Authors' Agents for an extract from the play *Mr Ellis Versus the People* by Jack Rosenthal. All rights whatsoever in this play are strictly reserved and application for performance etc. should be made before rehearsal to Margaret Ramsay Ltd, 14a Goodwin's Court, St. Martin's Lane, London WC2N 4LL; the Author, Suzanne Salimbene for an examination question from *Strengthening your Study Skills*, Univ. London Inst. Ed. 1982; the Author, John Small for an extract from 'The Crisis in Adoption' in *New Black Families;* Solo Syndications for the article 'Values that left a rape victim so vulnerable' by Sarah Tyne in *Mail on Sunday* 20.3.88; Tavistock Publications (Routledge) for poem 'A son must ... by R. D. Laing from *Knots;* Times Newspapers Ltd for extracts from the articles 'All those little white lies' by Brian James in *The Times* 11.4.88; 'Heroin ad campaign is a flop' by Brian Deer in *Sunday Times* 9.3.86, 'Complexities hold a real fascination' in *The Times* 22.5.86, 'Girls in poison coffee ploy' in *Times Educational Supplement* 28.2.86. All © Times Newspapers Ltd 1988, 1986; the Author, Victor Zorza for an extract from his article 'Village Voice' in *The Times* 2.6.86.

We have unfortunately been unable to trace the copyright holders of the articles 'Hippies "a band of brigands"' 'A Sporting Chance' by P. Mowbray, 'John McEnroe ...' by Richard Evans, extract from *Letter to a Teacher* by the School of Barbiana and would appreciate any information which would enable us to do so.

We are grateful to the following for permission to reproduce photographs and copyright material:

Copyright © Estate of H. M. Bateman, 1975, page 55; John Birdsall, page 6 *above left and right;* 'Child's Drawing', by permission of British Telecom and Bartle Bogle Hegarty Limited, page 87; Copyright © Steven Callahan/Abner Stein Agents, page 123; 'Reproduced by permission of the Cambridge Local Examinations Syndicate', pages 72 and 73; From '*Manwatching*', by Desmond Morris, published by Jonathan Cape Limited,